Carl Vernon Tower

The Relation of Berkeley's Later to His Earlier Idealism

Carl Vernon Tower

The Relation of Berkeley's Later to His Earlier Idealism

ISBN/EAN: 9783337042608

Printed in Europe, USA, Canada, Australia, Japan

Cover: Foto ©Thomas Meinert / pixelio.de

More available books at **www.hansebooks.com**

The Relation of Berkeley's Later to His Earlier Idealism

BY

CARL V. TOWER, A.M., Ph.D.,

INSTRUCTOR IN PHILOSOPHY IN THE UNIVERSITY OF MICHIGAN.

PRESENTED TO THE
FACULTY OF CORNELL UNIVERSITY FOR THE DEGREE
OF DOCTOR OF PHILOSOPHY.

ANN ARBOR:
1899.

ERRATA.

Page 7.   Note 1, read p. 176.
Page 12.   Note 5, read note 3, p. 47.
Page 13.   Note 1, read note 3, page 47.
Page 20.   Line 10, read muscle instead of muscular.
Page 55.   Line 29, read mists instead of midst.
Page 66.   Line 24, read Humian instead of human.

CONTENTS.

CHAPTER I.

§ 1. INTRODUCTION.

On one of the pages of Berkeley's Commonplace Book, the author notes that " nothing can be a proof against one side of a contradiction that bears equally hard upon the other." One might be inclined to admit that a just estimate of the Berkeleian philosophy resolves itself into this reflection, if it were not that historical evidence decidedly favors a more positive interpretation. Unfortunately, the true appreciation of the attitude adopted toward Reality by a philosopher who, like Berkeley, is not a system-maker —scarcely a systematizer of philosophic conceptions—is often partially obscured by the fact that the positive construction placed upon his work by subsequent thinking sometimes emphasizes the negative element of his philosophy, and so isolates it from the course of later philosophical development. This is a truism, but its explanation simply is that the spirit of philosophy respects the system by which its course of development is for a time apparently arrested. When theory succeeds theory in rapid succession, the progress of thought is in single file. A feature, an aspect, is sufficient to constitute a farther step in advance. The value of the theory is merely extensive, while that of the system is also intensive. The system serves always to recall the personality of the system maker, the theory is merged in its later outgrowths, apart from which it is abstract and featureless.

Berkeley was not the creator of a system. Rather was he a man with a theory of life, of morals, of Reality. Thus it is not surprising if, in his philosophy, the many definite tendencies in the direction of Empiricism have come to be regarded as almost the only positive elements in his conception of the world.[1] The history of philosophy makes evident the value of Berkeley as a link in the empirical succession from Locke to Mill, though with regard to his philosophy as a whole, it may likewise be said that Empiricism forms a negative rather than a positive element. The lines of thought followed by him in his earlier metaphysical undertaking are undoubtedly those which make most clearly and definitely toward the empirical views adopted by his successors. It

---

[1] " In its best known form, as a factor in the history of philosophy, only an empirical idealism." Burt: "A History of Modern Philosophy " (1892).

was, perhaps, unfortunate for the later acceptance of the Berkeleian theory of immaterialism, in a form more acceptable to its originator, that the 'new doctrine' found so ready an acceptance as to what have since been regarded as its essential features: The Cartesian dualism of thought and existence, so haltingly maintained by Locke[1] in his doctrine of substance, added to Berkeley's own nominalistic tendency and further sustained by his *religious* 're-pugnance' to an atheistical, unthinking 'matter', were the forces at work in the life of Berkeley, which early culminated in his view that, upon the existence or non-existence of abstract matter, there lay at stake the consistency of human reason with itself, and our only warrant for the objectivity of the ideals which human reason sets for itself. It may indeed be objected that these ideals, being so apparently of a theological cast, were the rocks and stubble which prevented the successful spading up of false notions und prejudices so vigorously begun. But as Berkeley does not lay claim to a philosophy without presuppositions, so neither does he regard the prepossessions of his opponents as in themselves obstacles to truth, provided only the motives underlying them be not inherently self-contradictory.

Whatever may have been the motive which determined Berkeley to become the promulgator of immaterialism, the discoverer himself seemed scarcely aware that the world was already ripe for his views. In the enthusiasm which formed the necessary accompaniment of the awakening consciousness of his mission in the world of philosophy, Berkeley was in part led to misconstrue the task which he had set for himself. Aware that he was to inaugurate a revolution in the current modes of metaphysical thinking, and mindful of the "mighty sect of men" which was to oppose him, the single problem of the existence or non-existence of matter assumed for him a size disproportionate to its true significance, in view of the other questions which an idealistic philosophy is called upon to solve. Immaterialism[2] is far removed from idealism in any positive and definite sense, though the former meant for Berkeley the latter, and accordingly upon the doctrine of the immateriality of matter—the first step in the idealistic progression which ensued, his early efforts are chiefly directed. The success which he attained in the clear and forcible series of arguments embodied in the Principles of Human Knowledge, was at the time grudgingly attested in comments, which, however, may best be expressed in the words of the more favorably disposed critic, Hume:

---

[1] Cf. T. H. Webb: "Veil of Isis," p. 12.

[2] "It is the negative side of his philosophy to which —unfortunately, but naturally—he was led in his early works to give the greatest relative consideration." Morris: "British Thought and Thinkers", p. 221.

Berkeley's arguments says he, "admit of no answer and produce no conviction."[1]

"But the lessons in scepticism which Hume drew from them were foreign, not only to the spirit and intention of Berkeley, but in not a few instances, even in his earlier philosophy seemed directly opposed to the mould in which it was cast. Berkeley certainly overshot his mark in his too vigorous insistence upon the sensuous character of all that we know; and in consequence the objectivity of thought relations, which any idealism of value must in some sense lay claim to discover, appear, indeed, in his philosophy as a background, but highly colored with theological notions. His idealism, being a theory rather than a system, the various aspects which it assumes are external to one another; yet one form of idealism drops out of sight, rather than is premeditatedly abandoned for another. He runs the whole gamut of idealisms from phenomenalism to what is in the end very like Platonic Realism. There is something kaleidescopic about this progression, one cannot say that there is any true line of demarcation between the earlier and the later, although the fundamental difference is apparent. Berkeley never deepens his conceptions to the extent of fully ascertaining if they are in agreement or non-agreement with the propositions which form the starting point of his early position.[2] Thus there results a number of seemingly heterogeneous lines of thought which are, in great part, rather suggestions and beginnings in thought than steps in a course of logical development. If, then, our interpretation shall endeavor to determine the resultant of these lines of thought it ought to effect this, not by a process of subjectively balancing the evidence for or against the earlier or the later theory as representative of Berkeley, but by taking such explicit utterances as he offers us in his general attitude toward philosophy other than his own. Berkeley has most frequently been regarded as an extreme Nominalist, and upon this basis largely rests the claim of Empiricism upon him as its representative. This Nominalism, whether of an extreme or, as some would have it, of a modified type, is best set forth in his discussion of Abstract

---

[1] Works; Hume IV, p. 181.

[2] "We may be "inclined to wonder," says Balfour in his biographical introduction to Berkeley's works, that a man who had done so much before he was thirty, had not done much more by the time he was sixty. * * * That he produced so little in his maturer years is doubtless due in part to temperament, and to the distraction of an unsettled and wandering life, but it must also be largely attributed to the almost total absence of intelligent criticism, either from friends or foes, under which Berkeley suffered throughout the whole period during which criticism might have aroused him to make some serious effort to develop or to defend the work of his youth." "The Works of George Berkeley,' edited by George Sampson, 1898.

Ideas, which constitutes his Introduction to the Principles of Human Knowledge, and it is accordingly with this work as a basis that we shall introduce the first of the topics in this discussion.

§ 2. ABSTRACT IDEAS.

(a) *Abstract Images.*

The philosophical discussions and dialogues of Berkeley everywhere abound in figures, and the effect of his metaphors is sometimes to make one think that the Platonism of his later years was indeed the undercurrent of his life. for a time obscured by the new discovery which attracted him in his youth. The predominating figure which, in his early philosophy, serves to clothe his conception of the world is that of the analogy of human language to a divine language, which forms the interpretable system of nature. Our failure to interpret correctly this divine nature-language is in a large measure owing to our lack of appreciation of the true function of human language.

Now Philosophers have generally regarded the paradoxes and inconsistencies that reason is wont to encounter in its search for metaphysical truth as due to the inherent weakness of our faculties which, being finite, are unable to "penetrate into the inward essence and constitution of things"[1] in themselves infinite. But "it is a hard thing to suppose right deductions from true principles should ever end in consequences which cannot be maintained or made consistent."[2] Human reason, we should think, ought, if unhindered, to yield more satisfactory conclusions to the problems which it has it self raised, and "we should believe that God has dealt more bountifully with the sons of men than to give them a strong desire for that knowledge which he had placed quite out of their reach."[3]

The errors to which the untrammelled exercise of reason has given rise have been attributed solely to the finitude of reason as such, and it has not yet been sufficiently pointed out that the most fruitful source of them is language. The flexibility of language, which adapts it to ordinary intercourse and the common business of life, becomes its chief difficulty when it is of necessity employed in the nicer discriminations of metaphysics. Here as everywhere the word is our master, or is likely to become so, if the relations which it bears to our reasoning be not definitely understood.

---

[1] Introduction to the Principles of Human Knowledge, § 2.
[2] Ibid. § 3.
[3] Ibid.

Usually the word may be said to signify a conscious process; frequently, also, it does not. In the former case a conscious content is the equivalent of the word, in the latter merely a cerebral process. "Fear, love, hatred, admiration, and disdain, and the like, arise immediately in the mind upon the perception of certain words, without any ideas coming between "[1]—or, on the other hand the word may arouse as its equivalent a more or less definite idea. Language has thus other uses than that of arousing conscious processes by coupling a word with a particular definitely recognized conscious content or idea, since the word may arouse to action or passion without the intervention of the idea. Thus we see that a word may stand for no idea at all, or it may stand for other particular ideas than that of which it serves as the sign in any particular instance.

But the adaptability of language to the demands made upon it by ordinary life render it impossible for a word, by means of a fixed definition, to correspond in every case to the same definite conscious content. The definition indeed serves to govern and restrict the corresponding idea to relations among other ideas to which the definition is also applicable; but it is not true that the word stands always for the same idea. The mistaken notion that every name has "one only precise and settled signification"[2] has occasioned the belief in abstract ideas or abstract notions from which has sprung much confusion in metaphysical thinking. Thus men have come to regard the concepts of qualities, or of beings, which include several coexistent qualities, as abstract ideas.

We are now in a position to see a little way into the difficulty which Berkeley finds with the 'abstract idea' of his opponents. Without attempting in this place to establish a rigid definition of the Berkeleyian idea, it may be noted that is is oftenest synonymous with the above acceptation of a particular, definite, recognizable content of consciousness. The freedom which Locke allowed himself in the definition of idea as, "whatever is the object of the understanding when a man thinks "[3] is a liberty which Berkeley does nothing to restrict. The two conditions which it seems are everywhere necessary to the idea are that it shall be (a) a content of consciousness, (b) recognized as a definite content of consciousness, i. e., perceived.

Now the abstract idea appears in Berkeley's eyes to be in the following anomalous position. As idea, it must be recognizable as a definite content of consciousness, but, as abstract, it must—so it is claimed—be different in kind from the particulars, out of which,

---

[1] Principles of Human Knowledge; § 20 of Introduction.
[2] Ibid. § 18.
[3] "Essay concerning Human Understanding." Introduction, § 8

by observation of their common likenesses, the abstract idea has been formed. What Berkeley seems to say to his opponents in his polemic against abstract ideas is in effect this: 'You tell me that there are such things as abstract ideas—that besides the ideas of sense, the ideas of imagination, the ideas "perceived by attending to the passions and operations of the mind,"[1] the ideas of memory, etc., etc., you have also ideas from which all particulars are excluded, and which, though relating to the particular ideas that may be subsumed under them, are not themselves particular. But if these ideas for which you contend are anything at all, they are recognizable by you as definite conscious contents, and are thus particular, and, in so far, like the other particular ideas which you have. You can accordingly describe them, and, having recourse to introspection, you must surely discover that all you have are particular ideas. By some of these ideas you may indeed denote numbers of other particular ideas—but nowhere will you find the thing you call abstract idea.'

If the foregoing is a correct interpretation of Berkeley's thought about abstract ideas, it is easy to see that his difficulty with them lay in the unimaginableness of such things. An abstract image is, as Fraser says, manifestly absurd.[2] Taken in this sense it is doubtful if Locke—whom Berkeley seems to have chiefly in mind—ever seriously contended for such a thing.[3] On the other hand, if Berkeley be not understood to have thus misconceived the doctrine of his opponent as grossly as ever Locke misconstrued Descartes' 'innate ideas,' the distinction between his own view and that of the upholder of abstract ideas is far less than is often supposed. For Berkeley by no means denies the possibility of there being general ideas. All he denies is that there are general ideas or general notions taken in the above sense of abstract images. Let us see if Locke's own description of abstract ideas may serve further to explain Berkeley's difficulties.

Locke says: "The use of words then being to stand as outward marks of our internal ideas, and those ideas being taken from particular things, if every particular idea that we take in should have a distinct name, names must be endless. To prevent this, the mind makes particular ideas received from particular objects to become general; which is done by considering them as they are in the mind such appearances—separate from other existences, and the circumstances of real existence, as time, place, or

---

[1] "Principles," § 1.

[2] Selections, p 19, note.

[3] Like Berkeley, "Locke has everywhere a sober dread of abstraction, and clings to the particular and concrete with a sense of the risk of losing the real in the emptiness of the universal." Locke's 'Essay'; Fraser's ed., vol. II, p. 101, note 2.

any other concomitant ideas. This is called abstraction, whereby ideas taken from particular beings become general representatives of all of the same kind; and their names general names, applicable to whatever exists conformable to such abstract ideas. Such *precise naked appearances in the mind*"—which Beckeley takes to mean images—"without considering how, whence, or with what others they come there, the understanding lays up (with names commonly annexed to them) as the standards to rank real existences into sorts, as they agree with these patterns, and to denominate them accordingly."[1]

Now this passage in which the doctrine of abstraction is explicitly set forth, does not of itself particularly favor Berkeley's interpretation of Locke, but the subsequent use which the latter makes of abstractions in which e. g. the idea of extension is treated as something which we possess apart from the idea of that which is extended, and the idea of hardness apart from that which is felt — these, coupled with the passage immediately following the one we have just quoted, in which it is said that "the having of general ideas is that which puts a perfect distinction betwixt man and brute," induce Berkeley to think that the having of abstract ideas means the possession of a faculty the existence of which man is not able to verify by direct introspection of himself or by observation of the way in which objects come to be recognized in consciousness of a lower order than his own. In one of the dialogues there is to be found this passage: "I understand that the several parts of the world became gradually preceivable to finite spirits, endowed with proper faculties."[2] If this may be accepted as a hint toward an indeal evolution or spiritual unfolding of nature,[3] it may be seen that Berkley would naturally rebel against the claim that man possesses a faculty so different in kind[4] from that belonging to animals of a lower order than himself, and so undesirable as an element of his own consciousness. The abstract idea, in the sense of abstract image—that indescribable something which is neither this nor that definite and particular thing, but which is set over against the other definite and imaginable contents of consciousness—an idea of this sort Berkeley claims it is impossible to frame.

(b) Universals.

It would be in a great measure to anticipate a discussion of the notion and its objects if we were at this point to dwell at length upon Berkeley's positive conception of universals. Yet a few

---

[1] Locke's Essay, Bk. II, Ch. XI, 9.
[2] "Philonous", 3d dialogue.
[3] Cf. also, "Siris," note 2 of Fraser's "Selection's," p. 343.
[4] Intro. to "Principles," § 11.

words may be sufficient to show that with the abstract idea, in any other sense than that of abstract image, he finds no very great difficulty. He regards the abstract image as an absurdity because, although a content of consciousness different in kind from particu lars, it, however, always reduces itself to particulars which it professes not to be. "But," says he, "it is to be noted that I do not deny absolutely there are general ideas, but only that there are any abstract general ideas; for, in the passage we have quoted wherein there is mention of general ideas, it is always supposed that they are formed by abstraction after the manner set forth in sections 8 and 9,"[1] which last "I do not think a whit more needful for the enlargement of knowledge than for communication."[2] "It is, I know, a point much insisted on that *all knowledge and demonstration are about universal notions*, to which I fully agree; but then it does not appear to me that those notions are formed by abstraction in the manner premised—*universality*, so far as I can comprehend, not consisting in the absolute, positive[3] nature or conception of anything, but in the relation it bears to the particulars signified or represented by it; by virtue whereof it is that things, names, or notions, being in their own nature particular, are rendered universal."[4]

Thus it is not the claim that we are able to generalize experience by means of "universal notions" to which Berkeley takes exception, but rather the claim, which rightly or wrongly he reads into Locke, "that those notions are formed by abstraction in the manner premised." And it is not so much the process of abstraction that he objects to as the hypostatization of the abstraction thus formed; for, thus hypostatized, it is the abstract image to which every element of particularity is denied. The abstract universal, in fulfilling its claim to be idea in consciousness, must have its sensuous aspect, and so must submit itself to the condition of being particular,[5] though a particular with a universal reference; but this necessary element of particularity is denied it by its claimants; hence the falsity and uselessness of such an idea. But it might be objected to Berkeley, this abstract universal has indeed a sensuous side, though the particularity of the idea does not necessarily follow from this, and consequently it is not what you claim it to be—an abstract image. Thus it is surely possible to form the idea of man in general which, *in the meaning that it has* for me, is

---

[1] Introduction to Principles of Human Knowledge, § 12.

[2] Ibid. § 15

[3] *i. e.* As an inflexible quasi-entity in the form of abstract image, having no relation to the particular to which it is presumably applicable.

[4] Introduction to Principles of Human Knowledge, § 15.

[5] v. note 2, p. 131 of this essay.

different from the particular fleeting images which accompany this
abstract idea; and, as the latter has for me this universal meaning,
it is in consciousness a something distinct from the particular. To
this we might, in behalf of Berkeley, ask in reply: Why then is it
not the case that, granted the same premises, we march straight to
the same conclusions? If we differ in our reasonings, is it not
because we differ in our experiences, and because, in consequence,
the sensuous images, which are only the obverse of the universals
we employ, necessarily have something to do with our conclusions?
In the Commonplace Book, Berkeley instructs an imaginary reader
as follows: "Let him not regard my words any otherwise than as
occasions of bringing into his mind determined significations . . .
I desire and warn him not to expect to find truth in any book or
anywhere but in his own mind." Our assurance of truth, he seems
to imply, is in the correspondence of the experiences of finite
beings; and hence, if we would have truth we must not neglect the
particular sensuous aspect of our experience, nor yet regard it as a
hinderance to the universal which it bears within it. Not that we
could ever attain truth by means of particulars which have no universal aspect, though every idea is indeed particular. "If we will
annex a meaning to our words and speak only of what we can conceive, I believe we shall acknowledge that an idea, which, considered in itself, is particular, becomes general by being made to
represent or stand for all other particular ideas of the same sort."
The idea, then, which is in itself definite and particular, the
image, and the conglomerate of particular experiences, has nevertheless a representative character in which may be seen the
evaluation by the rational consciousness of the particulars which
the image is taken to represent. That is, we are confined to particulars, Berkeley says; but particulars, at least some of them, have
a universal reference, this universal reference consisting in simply
recognizing that the general idea has no peculiarity which marks it
off as the special property of any particular idea.[1] Thus the idea
of a triangle is a general idea or notion, not "as if I could frame
the idea of a triangle which is neither equilateral, nor scalenon, nor
equicrural; but only that the particular triangle which I consider,
whether of this or of that sort it matters not, doth equally stand
for and represent all rectilinear triangles whatsoever, and is *in that
sense universal.*"[2]

As a conclusion of the matter we may, I think, fairly interpret
Berkeley as follows: In our thinking we are confined to particu-
tars i. e., there are not in our consciousness universals existing as
quasi-entities over against a number of particulars different from

[1] Cf. later discussions of the notion; also note 2, p.— of this essay.
[2] Introduction to the "Principles," § 15.

them in kind. The human mind is of the nature of a republic rather than of a monarchical system. On the other hand, the particularity of the idea is not its only aspect; for the universality of certain of our ideas at least is as true and immediately recognizable as the particularity which belongs to them all. If this is a fair interpretation of Berkeley, as we read this doctrine in the Introduction to the Principles of Human Knowledge, I see nothing that can justify the belief that he assigns a prior right to the particular as against the universal. Rather does it seem to be a plea for the equal rights of the universal and the particular, as distinguishable features of the idea.

But the importance of Berkeley's defense of the particular, as against the asserted existence of a featureless abstraction, must not, on that account, be minimized. He is here as elsewhere more often the champion of the particular than of the universal; and the impetuosity of his attack upon the territory usurped by his opponent doubtless prevented him from seeing that his own defenses were hastily constructed, sufficient for the occasion only, but not of a character to withstand the carefully planned attacks of later thought. Thus it comes about that "his defective views on this subject perplex his whole philosophy." Dr. James McCosh, no very friendly critic, says: "he rejects, as I believe he ought, abstract ideas, in the sense of Locke, that is, in the sense of images of qualities; and he claims it is his merit that he gets rid of grand abstractions . . . . . but, while he has exposed the errors of Locke, he has not established the positive truth . . . . . Had he taken as much pains in unfolding what is contained in ' considering ' a figure as triangular, and Peter as man, without considering other qualities, and what is involved in forming general propositions and reasoning about qualities, as he has taken to expel abstract ideas in the sense of phantasms, he would have saved his own philosophy, and philosophy generally from his day to this, from an immense conglomeration of confusion."[1] This is no doubt true; but it is not impossible that where, as in the case of Berkeley's philosophy, it is admitted on all sides that "an immense conglomeration of confusion " exists, a part of the confusion may be due to the neglect of certain strongly marked lines of thought in favor of others less prominent in his philosophy as a whole, but more clearly developed at certain stages of its progress. As Professor Wenley says: "Like Kant, Berkeley is not to be regarded in one aspect of his work only, and the same materials which viewed in a certain aspect, constitute in a large measure his value for philosophy should perhaps be viewed in another light, if we are to be true to the thought of the founder of idealism himself." [2]

[1] McCosh: " Locke's Theory of Knowledge with a notice of Berkeley " in Criteria of Truth, p. 57.
[2] " British Thought and Modern Speculation," in Scottish Review, Vol. 19.

CHAPTER II.

In the beginning which we have thus made in our attempted determination of the general Berkeleian conception of the world, his view of abstract ideas has been given the first place as the epistemological *motif* of that idealistic attitude toward Reality which Berkeley inaugurated. Partly on account of the natural limitations attaching to human language, partly because of the negligence of metaphysicians, who do not always verify the correspondence between the terms which they employ, and definite concrete thoughts, without which words are mere stumbling blocks in the way of logical thinking—it has come about that a kind of spurious currency was brought into circulation, which has not been without its effect upon the metaphysics of the past. It is Berkeley's professed task to recall men to a more adequate appreciation of the meanings that underlie the terms by which they designate supposed existences. "Nothing," says he, "seems of more importance toward erecting a firm system of sound and real knowledge, which may be proof against the assaults of scepticism than to lay the beginning in a distinct explication of what is meant by thing, reality, existence, for in vain shall we dispute concerning the ' real existence ' of things, or pretend to any knowledge thereof, so long as we have not fixed the meaning of those words."[1]

In this enquiry with which Berkeley sets out there may be found at least some feeble anticipation of that later "voyage of discovery" which was to tax the energies of a mightier intellect than his own. "'Tis on the meaning and import of existence that I chiefly insist." The metaphysical question: what is Reality? Berkeley is the first to raise explicitly in the form, what is the meaning of Reality or rather, we may say, what assignable meaning can we give to that which we call Reality, i. e. by what ideas can we designate the Real? The solution of this problem is partly foreshadowed in the very manner of stating the question itself. The Real must at least fulfill the negative condition of not being that which cannot be expressed or in some way verified in ideas. But then what are ideas?

For answer Berkeley unquestioningly sets out from the Cartesian separation of thought and existence, idea and thing. Reality was virtually comprehended under these two categories, and

---

[1] Principles of Human Knowledge § 89.

as the Lockian psychological theory of knowledge progressed it became more and more evident that these two heterogeneous quiddities would never fulfill the requirement of explaining one another, which had been implied in the assertion of their mutual relation. There was needed a bold stroke which would at once destroy the independence of thought or substance. The violent disruption of these two existents effected by Decartes must be succeeded by the summary relegation of one or the other to the rank of dependent existence. And there was no question as to which should ultimately yield precedence to the other. The unknown must ever derive its explanation from the known. Knowledge had been defined by Locke as the preception of the connexion and agreement or disagreement and repugnancy between our ideas. It only remained to discover whether or not ideas alone, and the knowledge we have by means of them, are in harmony with the ordinary preceptions of life and that partially organized system of truth of which we are made aware in the knowledge of the several sciences. An affirmative answer to this question would mean that ideas, hitherto conceived as subjective merely, and thus in separation from an unknown substance, must declare their adequacy to fulfill all the conditions of objectivity required by the scientific and ordinary naive consciousness. The objectivity of the idea once established, as idea it would yet retain its essential relatedness t) the percipient and cognitive consciousness, and thus maintain its position as an element in a system of conscious experiences. Cartesian substance could thus be banished to the limbo of useless metaphysical abstractions.

The obstacles in the way of the desired consummation which presented themselves to Berkeley were, in the first place, the prejudices of mankind, and second, the semblance of agreement between substance and ideas, which still remained in the Lockian epistemology as the formal assertion of a correspondence between ideas and the primary qualities of things.

With regard to the first difficulty, the long established prepossessions of men in favor of unthinking substance would naturally render them unfavorably disposed toward an abrupt reversal of their customary ways of thinking. Thus, until they could be brought to see that true objectivity does not necessarily imply the existence of an unknown or unknowable substance, and that ideas do not of necessity mean floating fancies and mere subjective creations of the mind, prejudice must be overcome by a review of the practical benefits conferred upon mankind by the Berkeleian "new discovery." Now, the extreme materialism of Hobbes and Gassendi, and the tendency towards the complete mechanical interpretation of everything, prevalent at the time of Berkeley, which, as he declares, is foreign to his nature, together with his own pious inclinations, brought it about that practical benefits were for him, in large part, synonymous with theological benefits. The result was that Berkeley fought the battle of Immaterialism with the Essay of Locke in one hand and the weapons of a deistic theology in the other. But, in the second place, as we have said, Locke's emphasis upon the ideal character of existence ill served to maintain a union between the primary qualities of substance and their ideal counterparts in the mind. The 'secondary qualities' had already taken their places in the ideal, which was also the knowable, system of experiences. Color, sound, heat, etc., many of the 'ideas' which go to make up the world of which we have actual experience, had already been declared subjective. The 'primary qualities,' five in number, extension, motion or rest, figure and number, together with impenetrability or solidity, were also 'ideas;' although supposedly the conscious effects of unknown coexistent causes. The only inlets into the "dark chamber of the understanding" were the senses; yet so far as concerned real knowledge of the world beyond consciousness, the senses were closed doors. The charge of subjective idealism would have been preferred against Locke had not Berkeley's own doctrine been at hand.[1]

The only egress from subjectivity lay in the recognition that all ideas of sense may, in one aspect, be viewed as subjective; while, in another aspect, it is equally true that they may be regarded as objective; and it is only in this way that objectivity of system, that is, rational knowledge, can declare itself. Thus we may, I think, understand Berkeley to say: If you have regard to an unthinking 'matter' or 'substance,' unknown or unknowable, independent of mind, I maintain that, in such a reference, ideas are subjective, mind-related things beyond which you cannot pass to supposed existences different from conscious facts. But if by 'objective' you mean the system of factual experience which we term the objective world, it is in that case the objectivity of the idea for which I contend; and furthermore, "I make extension, color, etc., to exist really in bodies independent of our mind." "You mistake me," he says in his third dialogue between Hylas and Philonous, "I am not for changing things into ideas, but rather ideas into things."

Primary qualities are then to be deposed from the position of independent existences and are to rank now with secondary qualities. But how effect this? They are useless assumptions, for, just as sound and color (subjective appearances) seem to be essen-

---

[1] For Locke's own approach to an idealistic position, Cf. e. g. T. II. Webb; Veil of Isis, passage above quoted, pp. 12-13. Also Locke's Essay: Bk. IV., Ch. II., 14; Bk. IV., Ch. XI., 1; Bk. IV., Ch. XI., 3; IV., XI., 8 (Cit. in " Veil of Isis ").

tially coexistent with the other objective aspects of our world of experience, so do the ideal counterparts of the primary qualities equally well fill up the manifold of objective experiences. Only the bare assertion remains that, corresponding to these ideal qualities, are their originals, presumably more real than they; the former being, as it were, photographs of the latter, shot into the mind, and preserving in some miraculous fashion the pristine beauty and truth belonging to the originals. But wherein lies the difference between these and the secondary; and why are not these latter also supposed to inhere in an unknown something beyond consciousness?

Now the primary qualities in their ideational character are referred to powers, secondary qualities to combinations of powers in an unknown substance. Accordingly the latter, although denominated by Locke 'simple ideas,' or simple elements of knowledge, are nevertheless, with reference to their origin in unknown combinations of 'powers,' complex; and it is because of their complexity that this class of ideas possess that distinctively ideal character which seems to belong to them and not to the 'primary qualities.' But how do we attain a knowledge of their complexity? By the introspection of conscious contents, of course, together with observation of the conditions under which we introspect; from which it appears e. g. that what is hot to one hand is cold to the other, or what is sweet to one palate may be bitter to another—requisite conditions being given. Thus you may refer secondary qualities to unknown combinations of powers, resident in one unknown substance if you will; but the real complexity of so-called mental elements is your test, and the condition under which your judgment is made, is relativity of the idea to the percipient organism. The *complexity of the experienced mental contents* is then the equivalent of their condemnation to rank also as independent entities by means of objective counterparts; and conversely, simplicity means the guarantee of their right so to exist. We have thus a sufficient criterion by which to judge of the validity of Locke's claim in behalf of primary qualities; and it is this task which Berkeley sets for himself in the Theory of Vision, though by no means attempting an exhaustive analysis of this class of ideas.

I.—IDEA AS MERE SENSATION.

Berkeley now proposes to turn the tables, and subject primary qualities also to the test of experience which, as we shall see, involves a reference of primary to secondary qualities. He wishes to test the less definitely known by the more completely known, rather than, with Locke, to refer the more definitely known to the more hypothetical. In the Theory of Vision the analysis of that class of ideas which have hitherto been regarded as simple elements of consciousness is undertaken with reference to Sight and Touch only, although the essay undoubtedly implies far more than that which is explicitly set forth as the design of the author, which is: "to show the manner wherein we perceive by sight the Distance, Magnitude and Situation of objects; also to consider the difference there is betwixt the ideas of Sight and Touch and whether there be any idea common to both senses."[1]

In the second book of the essay, Locke had shown that "we get the idea of space, both by our sight and touch," which, says he, "is so evident, that it would be as needless to go to prove that men perceive, by their sight, a distance between bodies of different colors, or between the parts of the same body, as that they see colors themselves."[2] "This space, considered barely in length between any two beings, without considering anything else between them is called distance."[3] Now it was the current theory, to which Locke gave countenance, that the spatial determination, distance is perceivable by the sense or sight regardless of the way in which it is perceived by touch, against which the first argument in the Theory of Vision was raised. The initial assumption underlying the series of arguments with respect to distance, is the common agreement that "Distance of itself, and immediately, cannot be seen. Distance not being immediately perceivable by sight and yet being perceived. it follows that it is "brought into view by means of some other idea, that is itself immediately perceived in the act of vision."[4] These other ideas are then merely 'signs' or suggestions by which distance is introduced into the mind as a conscious percept or idea. Against the view that the mind by a kind of natural geometry immediately perceives distance by the mathematical judgment of lines and angles; and also against another opinion held by writers on optics to the effect that the eye judges distance by the greater or less divergence of the rays transmitted from the object, Berkeley urges objections which may be briefly stated as follows: (1) There are no such mathematical perceptions, for introspection does not reveal a process of computation or comparison of lines and angles. (2) Lines and angles, being merely mathematical hypotheses, are not objectively existent. (3) If the foregoing mathematical judgments were involved in our preception of distance, they would yet be insufficient of themselves to explain the phenomena we are considering. For the idea of distance being mediated by other ideas we must necessarily have

---

[1] Theory of Vision, § 31.
[2] Locke's Essay; Bk. II, Ch. xiii, § 2.
[3] Ibid. § 3.
[4] Theory of Vision § 2.
[5] Ibid. § 11.

some regard to the latter in determining the composition of our perception of distance. Thus introspection will show us that ideas, or sensations as we might now call them, produced by the muscular movement of the eyeball, accompany the accommodation of the eye for nearer or more remote vision.

Again with regard to the phenomena of accommodation, Berkeley tells us that the perception of distance is aided by the ''strain sensations'' with which we correct the confused appearance of objects brought too near the eye. But besides these muscle sensations or 'visual ideas' or 'signs' accompanying the employment of the 'visive faculty,' there are also visible signs, such as the particular number, size, kind, etc , of the things seen; and all these are of use to us in the determination of distance. From the foregoing we may conclude, that a man born blind would, if he were subsequently enabled to see, receive an entirely new set of sensations, which would be mere mind-related symbols, but meaningless, until their significance was learned by means of asso ciating them with those sensations earlier formed in his experience. Now color, Berkeley is ready to assume, is the proper and immediate object of sight, and this, being a secondary quality, is not without the mind; whereas 'outness' or independence of the mind is ascribed to extension, figure, and motion. But extension is inseparable from color, and where extension is there too is figure and also motion. In proof of this, we have the experience that the appearance of an object alters with its proximity to or distance from the observer, this difference displaying itself in the degree of faintness of color and outline.

The conclusion now is that the strictly visual sensations, colors, refer us to tactual sensations, sensations of muscular effort experienced in the resistance which bodies offer to us, sensations of bodily movement and of the movement of bodily organs, and lastly, sensations of muscular effort experienced in going to the distant object. ''Ideas of space, outness, and things placed at a distance are not, strictly speaking, the objects of the sight; they are no otherwise perceived by the eye than by the ear.''[1] But it has come about in our experience that ideas of hearing are more easily separable from ideas of touch than are those of sight. We hear the footfall of a man walking upon the street and we readily recognize the ideal character of the experienced sound; but it is a more difficult matter to realize that the man whom we see arouses a totally different class of sensations from the man whom we touch. Yet it is nevertheless true that, just as familiar words immediately arouse in our minds meanings far different from the sounds which are also conveyed, but of which we are scarcely aware, ''so like-

---

[1] Theory of Vision § 46.

wise the secondary objects, or those which are only suggested by
sight, do often more strongly affect us, and are more regarded,
than the proper objects of that sense."[1]

As in the case of Distance, we find that Magnitude also is not
immediate but suggested. The 'lines and angles' argument is
reasserted to prove the immediacy of our preception of magnitude
by Sight independently of the sense of Touch; but, again, recourse
to introspection declares the experiential nature of judgments of
this kind. The magnitude of the visible object constantly changes
with change of distance between the real object and the observer;
therefore, when we speak of the magnitude or size of a thing, it
must be that we have reference to a more stable, tangible, magnitude.[2] Again with regard to the Measurement of Magnitudes, the
essentially relative and inconstant nature of visible Magnitude at
once declares its utility as a standard. It is not the merely visible
foot or visible yard that we adopt as the unit of linear measurement for these appear of different lengths according to their distance from the eye; but it is rather a constant and invariable, tangible, magnitude to which we appeal. In further support of Berkeley's contention that Magnitude is perceived in the same manner
as Distance, we are reminded that "what we immediately and
properly see are only lights and colors in sundry situations and
shades, and degrees of faintness and clearness, confusion and distinctness."[3]

The heterogeniety of the ideas of Sight and Touch is further
shown by an analysis of what is contained in the ideas of Position
or Situation. Experience teaches us that certain ideas of touch
go with certain other ideas of 'visible' things, and that, on the
occasion of the latter, an instantaneous and true estimate of the
situation of outward tangible objects is made. These two classes
of ideas are two entirely different kinds of experience. "That
which I *see* is only variety of light and colors. That which I feel
is hard or soft, hot or cold, rough or smooth. What similitude,
what connexion, have those ideas with these?" But some have
nevertheless asserted the imposibility of thus divorcing visible and
tangible ideas, urging as a reason the numerical identity of the
objects of these senses and the equality of the number as given
immediately in the visual idea. To this Berkeley replies that

---

[1] Ibid, § 51.

[2] NOTE: Throughout the essay, tangible magnitude, tangible idea, tangible
object, etc., mean for Berkeley real magnitude, real idea, real object. At this
juncture Berkeley enlightens us somewhat with regard to his apparent use of
"tangible ideas" as the ultimate sense data. The reason here given is the evident utility of such sensations for the perservation of the bodily organism, "they
are adapted to benefit or injure our bodies, and thereby produce in our minds the
sensations of pleasure or pain." Cf. § on Suggestion.

[3] "Theory of Vision," § 77.

number also is a "creature of the mind"[1] nothing fixed and settled, really existing in things themselves; whatever the mind
chooses to regard as one is a unit, and the same thing from another
point of view may be a manifold. We must learn the applicability
of number to visible as well as to tangible ideas. The confusion
between these two kinds of ideas has led to the above mentioned
difficulty about objects being painted inverted upon the retina yet
seen upright; for, relatively to the visible earth, the position of
the retinal object is correctly depicted, and relatively to the tangible earth, that with which we are concerned is only the outward
tangible object.

The conclusion with regard to Distance, Magnitude and Situation, warrants us in affirming the following proposition: "The
extension, figures, and motions perceived by sight are specifically
distinct from the idea of touch, called by the same name; nor is
there any such thing as one idea, or kind of idea, common to both
senses."[2] There is no idea common to both these senses, because
ideas of light and color, being the only immediate objects of sight,
are specifically distinct from ideas of touch, and in consequence,
Space, Distance, Magnitude, Extension and Motion[3] are suggested
mediate ideas.

But if Sight and Touch yield us two entirely different sets of
ideas, why do we denote by the same name these groupings of different ideas? Furthermore, why are these ideas so mingled together in our experience as to seem inseparable? The answer to
both these questions is: In the course of our experience it has
come about that Visible and Tangible ideas have been constantly
associated together so that one has become the mark or sign of
the other. Thus a visible square suggests a tangible square
because, having learned the applicability of number to both sets of
ideas, we see that one resembles the other in having a corresponding number of parts or marks. But this 'sign language', whereby
visible ideas suggest tangible ideas, has been learned early in our
experience; and there has thus resulted the constant confusion
between them. The perception of an external world is apparently
immediate, experience having brought about such facility in the
interpretation of signs; but because of this, we are led to the
wrong inference that this immediateness is due to the sense of
sight alone, whereas by that sense we are made aware of colors
only, in varying degrees of light and shade.

It is now time to enquire more particularly into the nature of

---

[1] "Principles," § 12.

[2] "Theory of Vision," § 127.

[3] NOTE: That visible and tangible motion have nothing in common follows
as a corollary from the difference between visible and tangible extension—*vide* §
137. "Theory of Vision."

the Berkelian idea as set forth in the preceding sections of the
Theory of Vision. On the way to this we may note the definition
that occurs in § 45 of the Essay in which it is said: "I take the
word *idea* for any immediate object of sense or understanding
—in which large signification it is commonly used by the moderns." This statement, however, is made with reference to "tangible ideas" only. In its scope it is equivalent to the Lockian idea
and also to Berkeley's ordinary use of the term. As so extended,
it has not properly been the object of our consideration. It is
true that the above definition is inclusive of the narrower meaning.
in which the word 'idea' has been used throughout the Theory of
Vision, but it is with this restricted use that we are here concerned.

And I think it cannot fail to be readily understood from the
foregoing brief consideration of the essay that 'idea' is throughout
used in the narrower meaning of mere sensation. The proper
objects of sight are colors, just as the proper objects of hearing
are sounds, but in the perception of any external object there is
more involved than the mere sense-presentation of color. The
object presented in perception possesses 'outness,' extension and
figure, is, in short, externalized in space in a way that cannot be
accounted for by reference to the mere data of sight alone. The
true object of perception is therefore mediately constituted by·
means of these visual data, which serve as signs or suggestions of
tactual and muscular sensations, to which the last appeal is made.
On the other hand, the true object of sight is a mere mind-dependent sensation, colors—our sole visual data—being admittedly only
in the mind. Extension, figure and motion, three of Locke's primary qualities, are so far as concerns their reference to the visual
faculty, reduced to a condition of mind-dependency—a result
which Berkeley practically achieves here in the Theory of Vision.
Number, another of Locke's primary qualities, has also been declared a creature of the mind. With the disposal of figure, extension and distance in space, the perception of solidity, by means of
the visual faculty alone, is declared impossible. But the primary
qualities nevertheless reappear in another form, for tangible extension, magnitude, figure, etc., yet remain. It is true they are denominated "tangible ideas"; and are regarded as subjective, sensations, as in the case of "visual ideas"; but for all that they are
looked upon as ultimate data, beyond which we cannot pass. The
externality of the world remains for us an irreducible fact, as far
as the Theory of Vision is concerned; and visual ideas are related
to tangible ideas as signs to the thing signified.

But though we may as yet determine nothing further with
regard to tangible ideas, it is possible that additional light may be
thrown upon the Berkelian conception of visual ideas. We have
seen that, throughout the essay, idea is synonymous with sensa-

tion; but in what acceptation shall we take this equivalent term—
sensation? Is it a recognized conscious content; or is it an unre-
cognized and subconscious datum? Although here as elsewhere
Berkeley's theory of knowledge is undeveloped and fragmentary,
we may, I think, find a justification for holding to the latter of the
two constructions indicated as possible. For, in the first place,
idea, we have been told, may have another function than that of
arousing its precise equivalent in consciousness. Thus, the sensation of color may suggest other sensations; though color may
not be consciously recognized as present in the percept. Again,
our visual sensations have, in the upbuilding of our conscious experience, become so inextrically interwoven with their suggested
tangible sensations, that it is only by attention to the physiologi-
cal processes underlying the phenomena of vision that we can obtain a just estimate of what may be attributed to the functioning
of that 'faculty' alone. But we never perceive mere colors, i. e.,
mere visual sensations; or 'ideas'; for what in our perception we
are actually conscious of are colors extended, figured, etc. Visual
sensations, then, although necessary to the explanation of the
growth of our experience by means of their association with other
sensations, are strictly not perceived. This is the conclusion
reached in the Vindication of Theory of Vision[1] in which we are
told that the colored point "projected in the fund" of the eye is
unperceived. It is "tangible and apprehended only by imagination" i. e., it is a sign or 'suggestion' of other ideas with which
our knowledge of the outer world seems more intimately concerned.

<h2 style="text-align:center">II—IDEA AS PERCEPT.</h2>

The Theory of Vision to which we have referred in order to
obtain Berkeley's earliest acceptation of 'idea' was, as Fraser
says, the "opening wedge" which served to introduce the doctrine of Immaterialism as set forth in the Principles of Human
Knowledge. Little fault has been found with Berkeley for having
left so much of the work of associational psychology to be per-
formed by his successors; yet during the year which elapsed between the publication of the Theory of Vision and the appearance
of the Principles, we must assume that the work of associational
psychology had considerably advanced. So far as concerned the
Essay, we were left with the literal fact of tangible sensations, as
ultimate sense criteria of objectivity. But the notion that tangible sensations are really more ultimate than any other we must now
suppose to be a 'vulgar error,' which it was not Berkeley's pur-

---

[1] "Theory of Vision Further Indicated and Explained," § 50; Fraser's note
to § 3, "Theory of Vision," p. 168 of "Selections."

pose to examine and refute in a discourse concerning Vision. The
latter is merely an experiment, pursued a little way for the purpose
of satisfying himself with his new conception of objective existence, and further investigation along that line is no longer of para-
mount interest to him.

We are accordingly invited to take a fresh start with sensations, as it were, all on the same level. Analysis of the meaning
of supposed objective, mind-independent qualities (so far as we
were concerned with them in the Theory of Vision) has everywhere revealed their essentially composite character, and each one
of those units into which they resolve themselves declares itself in
consciousness as mind-dependent, a sensation. In short, when we
look to the meaning of objective existence in any of its particular
qualities, a sensation, in conjunction with some other sensation,
offers itself to us as the readiest and most complete explanation of
the quality. It seems we must conclude that all we have are these
ideas or sensations. In sensation, we have apparently come in
touch with Reality. We have now a fairly complete psychological
theory of knowledge; and we wish to discover the extent of its usefulness in metaphysic. We are no longer concerned with the
question of whether qualities of the object may be explained in
terms of sensation, but whether the object itself, in all the ways in
which it appeals to our sense-perception and cognitive consciousness, may be accounted for by means of the same sensations.

Now, with regard to the object, there is the commonly accepted opinion that by it we denote an existent which has a peculiar reality of its own, distinct from its being perceived. But if we
attempt to describe any natural object apart from its relation to
others, we can only describe it as it affects us; i. e., each special
determination of the object is seen to be some one or other of
the special revelations of sense. "The table I write on I say
exists, that is, I see and feel it; furthermore if I were out of my
study I should say it existed—meaning thereby that if I was in my
study I might perceive it, or that some other spirit actually does
perceive it." What more can be said of the existence of an object
than this? The object is a mere plexus of sensations, "and as
several of these are observed to accompany each other, they come
to be marked by one name and so to be reputed as one Thing."
These clusters of sensations give to us all the meaning that is contained in the 'existence' of the Thing. Beyond the Thing, as so
constituted, there is nothing. Some indeed, on the basis of a
distinction between the above mentioned primary and secondary
qualities, assert the existence of an object independent of sense
perceptions; but this can be no longer maintained, if, as will be
seen by reference to the Theory of Vision, primary may be equated
with secondary qualities. And after all, "it is but looking into

your own thoughts, and so trying whether you can conceive it possible for a sound, or figure, or motion, or color, to exist without the mind or unperceived."[1] Ideas cannot then be taken in any sense as copies of external things, for the external thing and the idea would of necessity be identical. If the orginals are perceived they are ideas; if unperceived, then that which is perceived is identical with that which is unperceived—a manifest contradiction.

Thus far with regard to the ordinary common sense distinction between thing and idea, as also the further distinction between object and percipient consciousness by means of supposed qualities inherent in the former. But in addition to the foregoing ways of conceiving the object, philosophers have asserted the existence of 'matter' variously regarded as 'substratum,' 'occasion,' 'substance,' to which the knowledge of our ideas and their relations to them, admittedly ideal, is ultimately to be referred. Now, aside from the uselessness of such a conception for purposes of explaining our experience, matter in this sense is in itself contradictory; for either it is something out of all relation to ideas, in which case it is unknowable and even its existence cannot be asserted, or else it is the things which we see and touch and handle, and thus a complex of sensations. If we are careful always to use words in their proper significations, that is, if we admit no term for which we cannot discover a definite mental equivalent, it is plain that we must reject the materialistic hypothesis of an "inert, senseless, unthinking substance," as self-contradictory because lending itself to no idea that we can frame of its existence. But, if on the other hand, by matter is meant merely the things present to us in external preception, Berkeley says that he finds no great difficulty with the term. "I do not argue against the existence of any one thing that we can apprehend either by sense or reflection. That the things I see with my eyes and touch with my hands do exist, I make not the least question. The only thing whose existence we deny is that which Philosophers call Matter or corporeal substance."[2]

Our knowledge seems then only in a sense to be confined to existences which are merely subjective. We are, indeed, Berkeley tells us, confined to ideas or phenomena, and "to explain the phenomena, is all one as to show why, upon such and such occasions, we are affected with such and such ideas."[3] But, on the other hand, the distinction between ideas as things, and ideas as mere creations of the mind, appears for Berkeley to keep its full

---

[1] Principles of Human Knowledge § 22.

[2] Principles § 35; repeated frequently in the dialogues between Hylas and Philonous.

[3] Principles of Human Knowledge § 50.

significance. "There is a *rerum natura* and the distinction between realities and chimeras retains its full force."[1] For after all
we have been considering the object in one of its aspects merely.
The object has been shown to be resolvable into a complex of sensations, and is thus a percept or idea. But these sensations are
for Berkeley only the hypothetical conscious elements into which
the percept is ideally resolvable, and its existential nature is by no
means exhausted. The object of perception has been called idea
"because," as Berkeley tells us in the third dialogue between Hylas
and Philonous "a necessary relation to the mind is understood to
be implied by that term." But this does not of necessity mean
that it is not likewise dependent for its existence upon something
beyond the individual consciousness in which it is held.

Now Locke has found that in order to determine the nature
of certain of our ideas, viz., those complexes of sensation, or per-
cepts which we have been considering, we must take into account
the causal origin or source of these simple ideas of which the percept (as we shall now call it) is made up. The percept in other
words has a reference beyond itself, it can only be defined by
something that is in a certain sense not itself; to understand its
complete nature, we must recognize that its being is not wholly
subjective, but dependent also upon something objective. We
have seen that powers residing in an unknown 'corporeal substance' were supposed by Locke to fulfil, the condition of supply-
ing this need for something objective by reference to which ideas
of sense could be explained. But these powers being conceived
as objective counterparts of ideas, no distinction remained between
ideas and their counterparts. This Berkley has pointed out with
the conclusion that, as "an idea can be like nothing but an idea,"[2]
a mind dependent thing like nothing but a mind-dependent thing;
so all things that we know involve a reference to percipient consciousness. Thus, that objective something has been wrongly conceived, for true objectivity means, not objectivity of mind to something which is *ex hypothesi* different from it, but objectivity of
mind, by means of the double reference of the percept, to mind and
to objective Being—as also Mind.

Nor is it apparent—to dwell somewhat at length upon this
point—that the Berkelian percept or thing is, in its total character,
entirely comprehended in the psychological description of the
bundle of sensations which compose it; and that the causal reference of the percept to objective existence is a mere artifice by
which to escape solipsism. It is not as though, by defining the

[1] Principles of Human Knowledge § 34.
[2] Vid. Ueberweg's discussion of this point (Annotations to "Berkeley's Prin-
cipien," trans. in Krauth's "Principles of Human Knowledge," p. 343.

object in terms of sensation, one were thereby precluded from the recognition that objects involve a reference beyond the individual consciousness, any more than, in regarding the object as throughout constituted by thought-relations, one would be taken to imply the categories which he as an individual finds it convenient to employ in thinking of the object. What Berkley means is rather the universal character which attaches to the percipient as well as to the cognitive consciousness—the universality of sense-perception as an element not to be neglected in our explanation of experience. Again, it is not as though a mass of sensations were thrust into the mind, and the door closed upon all objective existence; but we first define the object as having a necessary reference to percipiency, and then, from the dual character of mind-related existents, as objects of sense and objects of imagination or memory, etc., arrive at the distinction of mind and mind. The objective character which necessarily belongs to the peculiar nature of the thing or percept cannot consistently be conceived as matter; it must then be conceived in analogy with that to which the percept has been shown to have a necessary reference, i. e. mind. How well Berkeley succeeds in thus substituting objective mind for objective matter is another question. All that we are here concerned to set forth is his insistence upon a fundamental distinction between ideas; and that the understanding of idea as percept involves a consideration of its reference to other than the individual percipient mind. Accordingly we shall now briefly discuss the Berkelian idea in connection with a second class of Things which he denominates mind or spirit.

3—SPIRIT, PHENOMENA AND IDEA.

In section 89 of the Principles we are told that our knowledge is not entirely confined to ideas, that "the term *idea* would be improperly extended to signify everything we know or have any notion of." For, "besides all that endless variety of ideas or objects of knowledge there is likewise something that knows or perceives them."[1] This perceiving, active being is what I call Mind, Spirit, Soul or Myself "—"that which I denote by the term I—which is neither an idea, nor like an idea, but that which perceives and wills, and reasons about them."[2] It is to this active perceiving principle that all the objects of sense must ultimately be referred for their explanation since, as Berkeley has told us, the reason for using the term idea rather than object is that there is thereby implied a necessary relation to the mind. Accordingly, if there are recognizable differences in the ideas which the mind possesses, it

---

[1] Principles of Human Knowledge § 2.
[2] Principles of Human Knowledge § 139.

may be possible to discover wherein this consists, not by the reference of ideas to a material substance, but by the relation which seems to subsist between them and the active, perceiving mind.

Now all ideas are divided into three classes: "ideas actually imprinted on the senses; or else such as are perceived by attending to the passions and operations of the mind; or lastly, ideas formed by help of memory and imagination—either compounding, dividing, or barely representing those originally perceived in the aforesaid ways."[1] All ideas, however, regarded as mere objects of consciousness, are in themselves passive—"there is nothing of Power or Agency included in them."[2] With regard to certain of these there seems to be involved the creative or combining activity of mind; for "I find that I can excite ideas in my mind at pleasure and vary and shift the scene as often as I think fit"[3] and "this making and unmaking of ideas doth properly denominate the mind active."[4] But over another class of ideas, viz., those of sense, I find that I have no control. These have a strength, a liveliness and distinctness which do not belong to the ideas of the imagination. They are chiefly to be distinguished from ideas that are purely subjective by the fact of their appearing in an orderly and coherent series, and also because of their entire independence of the will. However, these ideas like all others are passive and mind-dependent, they have no being apart from percipient mind. If, then, the nature of these ideas, in distinction from those of memory and imagination, is such as to warrant us in affirming their objective reference—since they are not wholly dependent upon individual mind—we are led to conclude their dependence upon *other mind*. "They are not generated from within by the mind itself"[5] and are therefore imprinted upon it "by a spirit distinct from that which perceives them[6], or "there is some other Will or Spirit that produces them."[7]

We may now summarize Berkeley's finding with regard to idea, so far as it has been considered in the present and preceding sections. It is (1) the mere atomic element of consciousness or sensation; (2) the object of external perception, or bundle of sensations, or percept, as we have chosen to call it, of whose being relation to percipient mind is a necessary condition; (3) this same object of external perception or percept in the being of which there is also involved a necessary

1 " Principles," § 1.
2 Ibid § 25.
3 Ibid § 25.
4 Ibid.
5 Ibid § 90.
6 Ibid.
7 Ibid § 29.

dependence upon *objective* mind. Gradually as the philosophy of Berkeley progresses, the term phenomenon [1] is substituted for idea, but if, in our interpretation, we discard the latter and adopt the new term, the two-fold meaning which may be given to the 'phenomenon' must be borne in mind. On the one hand 'phenomenon' implies for Berkeley a reference backward to the elemental conscious facts which make up its being, on the other hand there is in it implied a reference forward to objective consciousness.

In truth, the object and the sensation are the same and cannot therefore be abstracted from each other." [2] This was Berkeley's answer to the Cartesian dualistic hypothesis. As the object and sensation can only be ideally separated, we must interpret one in terms of the other. Thus, upon the direct evidence of conscious experience, we have partially carried out this programme as witnessed in the fact that the object is resolvable into sensation. But it would be a misinterpretation of his principle if we were to stop at this single and one-sided application; for if the object and sensation are only ideally separable, it seems not an illegitimate method of procedure to insist that, as sensational character is always necessary to the being of an object, so also sensation possesses a true objective character which cannot rightfully be denied it.

In order to exhibit these two equally necessary views of the phenomenon, their mutual relation would have to be shown; but this would involve a discussion of the Berkelian 'relations' between ideas, the third of the objects of our knowledge, and this we have reserved for the succeeding chapter, as also the more complete determination of his view of the self and objective mind, for upon this depends in large part the adequacy or inadequacy of the hypothesis which he substitutes for Cartesian "corporeal substance." All that we are concerned with here is the determination of the various meanings in which Berkeley uses idea. This we have seen, in one of its aspects, viz., from the point of view of its objectivity, involves a reference to Things to which in the present chapter we

---

[1] One of Ueberweg's objections to Collyn's use of 'phenomenon' rather than 'idea,' in his interpretation of Berkeley, is that the term phenomenon denotes a *complex* of sensations. (Annotations; Krauth's "Principles," p. 331). I cannot avoid thinking, however, that idea is more often used in the later works for the composite, the phenomenon, rather than for the object of the special senses. Another of Ueberweg's objections is that the "word *Erscheinung* presupposes a thing-in-itself of which it is the phenomenon." Now with all Berkeley's zeal in disclosing to us the 'new doctrine' that the senses report truly an external world, with all his eagerness in demonstrating the non-existence of 'unknown substance' this insistence upon the *esse-is-percepi* should not conceal the fact that for Berkeley the being of the phenomenon is grounded upon something other than the individual consciousness. The thing-in-itself is, in short, the content of the divine consciousness, an unknown but not an unknowable.

[2] "Principles," § 5.

shall attempt to assign no precise signification. For the present we shall content ourselves with the simple recognition that the being of the phenomenon is in part dependent upon the Will of a more powerful Spirit than the finite, viz., God, who is able to produce in the latter the regular and orderly series of phenomena which constitute the objective system of Nature.

In the Theory of Vision, we saw that ideas as sensations were merely the signs which enabled us to become aware of other sensations; and, further, we saw that sensations always come to us in groups. It is the extended, colored, tangible thing that we actually meet with in our experience, rather than the mere sensation. The latter, as it were, receives its being merely from the fact of its being one of a manifold. This truth was expressed, in the case of visual signs, by instituting an analogy of visual signs with those of human language, colors i. e. mere visual sensations, together with their variations of light and shade, make up for us a sort of visual sign-language or "Universal Language of Nature." In the Principles, however, in which, it is true, the sensationalistic or empirical view is brought to a completion and throughout emphasized, it is also apparent that this "Universal Language of Nature" is of supersensous' or extra human origin. The phenomenal object or intuited manifold of sensations in turn receives its complete explanation not only in the sensations of which it is made up but by its objective reference to something other than itself. As sensations are significant of the object, as by them we are taught to expect the possible future sensations in the groups constituting the object of external perception, so on the other hand is the phenomonal object itself representative of a Divine order of Nature with regard to which the phenomenon is merely the significant sign. It is this second meaning of ideas that occasions the frequent use of the word phenomenon in the dialogues of Berkeley and particularly in Siris.

Viewed from the standpoint of the Berkelian idea, the altered meaning which it receives by being regarded as phenomenon is one of the chief features which distinguish the later philosophy of Siris from the earlier standpoint of the Theory of Vision and the Principles. In the latter work phenomenon and Idea, rather than sensation and percept claim our attention.

In the Principles of Human Knowledge. "Idea" and "archetype" receive only a brief treatment at Berkeley's hands. In this work, as we know, his chief insistence was upon the impossibility of the existence of abstract matter in any of the significations in which it had hitherto been maintained by the philosophers. Accordingly, at this point,[1] having considered various

---

[1] "Principles of Human Knowledge," § 71.

other meanings of matter, he briefly dismisses the notion of archetypal ideas, understood as quasi-material forms, independent of the
Divine mind, and in accordance with which the latter creates the
world.[1] The constitution of the world must throughout conform
to that type of reality which, as it enters into our experience, we
variously denote by the terms mind, or self or spirit; and archetypes of our own ideas, if such be admitted, can exist only in *some
other mind.*[2]

But that there are certain unknown Ideas in the Mind of God
—archetypal forms not independent of his will—Berkley does not
deny. Indeed his later philosophy moves almost exclusively in
the region of these Platonic existences. This does not mean however that the earlier empirical standpoint is now abandoned, but
only that there is a greater insistence upon the objectivity of the
idea which we have before noticed. In this latter aspect, the reality of the thing or phenomenal object is seen to depend not only
upon its relation to percipient mind; its complete reality can only
be understood by reference to universal, creative mind. Accordingly Berkeley is brought to the fuller recognition of an archetypal
system of forms, Ideas, or Divine meanings, of which the phenomenal object is merely the significant sign. For "do I not acknowledge " says he in the third dialogue between Hylas and Philonous
"a two-fold state of things—the one ectypal or natural, the other
archetypal and eternal? The former was created in time, the latter existed from everlasting in the mind of God." In Siris the
discovery of this archetypal system by means of interpretable
sense-given phenomena, is regarded as the true end of all human
endeavor.

But the archetypal form or Idea, although certainly indicat-
ing a much closer affiliation to the Platonic philosophy than is discoverable in any of Berkeley's earlier works, cannot be identified
with Idea in the strictly Platonic sense of the word. For it is
with Berkeley equivalent to the "notion," which in our discussion
of the Introduction to the Principles of Human Knowledge we
took to be his recognition of the conceptual character that attaches
to ideas. If we read this later doctrine in the light of his earlier
work, idea does not appear to us as the vague and shadowy rem-
iniscence of an intangible universe of pure forms, from which we
are cut off, save by the negation of sense-reality and the indulgence
of the contemplative and speculative mood. Rather is it the case
that the Berkelian world appears here and now, with the noticeable
difference between the earlier and later construction of it, that the
conceptual is at last accorded the just recognition which was ever

---

[1] Fraser; "Philosophy of Berkeley," Blackwood series pp. 350–353.
[2] "Principles," § 99.

implied in Berkeley's insistence upon the objective nature of the idea, as of equal importance with its subjective reference. Objective and subjective are alike aspects of the phenomenon, the thing present to perception. In this objectivity of the idea we have one of the elements by which the antithetical poles of Berkeley's philosophy, his earlier empiricism and later Rationalism, are united in the thought of a spiritual unfolding of Nature in which we pass by gradual steps from the mere sense-given phenomena to the Ideas of imminent law and order, goodness and moral government, in the absence of which imminent Ideas of Reason there would be for us no world, but chaos.

To treat otherwise than in this brief fashion these objects of human knowledge which, because of their changed notation, appear in Siris as new elements foreign to the earlier thought of Berkeley, would be to run too far afield upon ground which should more properly be covered in our subsequent enquiries. We have so far attempted to show, not without the cost of some tedious but necessary repetition, the various meanings which Berkeley assigns to the word idea. In the interest of clearness, I subjoin the following summary at the close of this chapter:

1. Idea is used as object of the special senses, sound, color, touch, etc.; but color is never perceived except as something colored and extended; touch is always the feeling of something resisting and possessing form. Consequently single objects of the special senses are never true objects for us, i. e. perceived. Idea in this first sense is then 'mere sensation'.

2. Idea as the immediate object or phenomenon of perception, resolvable into particular sensations and consequently dependent for its being upon percipient mind. Idea as such is the complex of sensations, marked by one name, and so regarded as a thing.

3. Idea in the foregoing sense, but distinguished from the subjective contents of the individual consciousness, and thus regarded as dependent upon objective mind.

4. Idea as archetype, Platonic idea or Notion. Or we may express it thus:

1. idea = 'mere sensation'.

2. idea = phenomenon $\begin{cases} \text{a. as complex of sensations.} \\ \text{b. as conceptual, and in this latter} \\ \quad \text{sense the equivalent of:} \end{cases}$

3. Idea as Notion.

A concluding word with regard to these three classes in order to free from ambiguity these various meanings of the word idea, may be necessary, and may serve to acquaint us in advance with some of the difficulties we are likely to encounter in our farther review of Berkeley's interpretation of experience. In the first place, idea as 'mere sensation' seems grossly at variance with his frequently repeated assertions that ideas are particular, definite, discoverable mental contents. I am also of the opinion that idea is most frequently used by Berkeley in the sense of phenomenon, i. e. it implies more than the sensations which constitute it actually reveal in perception. In fact it is never the ·mere sensation' when the idea is consciously perceived. But the phenomenon, it was in part Berkeley's mission to tell us, is in every case resolvable into those units; and, as it is only the complex that is perceived, it seems that in his earlier philosophy Berkeley does have reference to these atomic elements of consciousness or hypothetical sensations. The phenomenon, as a complex of sensations, needs no further notice here; but to the phenomenon in its objective reference, attach, in one form or another, most of the difficulties we are likely to encounter in the following chapters. And, as a tentative step, we take the philosopher's word for it that in doing away with Locke's 'abstract material substance', he has merely denied the causal reference of sense objects to such substance, while, in doing this, by showing the necessary relation to percipient consciousness of all such objects, he has not thereby affected the object, or denied to it all causal reference to objective existence, but has merely substituted mind for matter.

The question which is thus raised for us is: What is the nature of the Divine Being which Berkeley thus substitutes for substance? Is it a deistically conceived contrivance, artificially introduced to escape subjectivity and support theistic belief, or is his view of the personality of God and man the rationally grounded consequence of a new meaning which he gives to 'idea'? Again, is the order, steadiness and regularity which he ascribes to the ideas of sense, thereby distinguishing them from subjective fancies, consistently maintained in a philosophy which seems to destroy the ground on which it stands by the acknowledgment that all ideas are particular? And, finally, in the archetypes or Ideas of Reason which occupy so bold a position in Siris, do we encounter importations foreign to the life current of Berkeley's thought, or are we here only brought to a better understanding of less familiar but none the less important elements in his early theory of knowledge? If the philosophy of Siris merely represents a platonizing mood into which Berkeley fell in his declining years, there is no discoverable relation between his earlier negative and his later positive idealism. But if the Idea, which seems in Siris the instrument and motive by which he reaches his final conclusions is affiliated, as we have suggested, to other elements of his earlier works, we may not be forced to a decision between Empiricism and Rationalism which will be altogether without evidence in support of the latter and less frequently accepted view.

CHAPTER III.

1. *Relations.*

a. Arbitrary Connection

A third of the objects of human knowledge are relations. We have thus far instanced the various meanings in which Berkeley used the word idea in the earlier and later phases of his idealism, and we have now to consider the manner of their connection. In the first place, we may again note that the *point d' appui* which served to introduce Berkeley into his new idealistic universe was the reduction of Locke's primary qualities to the secondary, thereby equating all the sensations derived from the special senses. This constituted his negative disproof of matter. So far as concerned the existence of 'abstract matter', the testimony of the senses at any rate could not be alleged in its behalf. But matter had been regarded as the cause, if not primary, at least the causal agent, and idea the effect. Accordingly in the absence of matter and the consequent denial of a material cause it results that any phenomenal object or any object of the special senses is, in itself, regarded as particular, inactive, destitute of power or causal agency.

Now the principle of cause and effect may be for us an original, underivative revelation of the rational consciousness[1]; and this is by no means denied, for in the second dialogue between Hylas and Philonous the latter is made to say: 'I do by no means find fault with your reasoning in that you collect a cause from the phenomenon, but I deny the cause deducible by reason can properly be termed matter.' But, on the other hand, if causal agency can no longer be attributed to the objects of sense, since they are now phenomena; and since the combining and relating activity, in so far as that may be attributed to the mere individual consciousness, does not extend to these ideas of sense; we must discover some other connection, by means of which the presence of the phenomenon may be accounted for and the nature of the cause revealed to us.

Now, in the process of introspectively analyzing the contents of consciousness, we found that the ideas obtained by one sense are translatable into terms of another sense. But we further dis-

---

[1] Fraser; "Berkeley," Blackwood Philos. Classics, p. 198.

covered that the objects of one sense are, so far as we can see, totally unlike those of another. True, the very process which serves to display their heterogeneity exhibits also—because of the parallel discovery of their interpretability in terms of each other—the mind-dependence of all objects of consciousness. Yet, introspection stops short of telling us *why* the objects should be interpretable in terms of others unlike them. There is then, *for us*, no discoverable necessary connection between ideas.[1] But we can no longer explain the phenomenal object in terms of matter; and mind, if it cannot discover to us the *why*, may at least serve to exhibit the *how* of the connection.

This Berkeley proceeds to show by instituting the parallelism between sense symbols and words, the significant signs of human speech. In the latter case, words have no similarity to the meanings which they serve to convey, to the sound waves or the nerve processes by which the result is brought about. That sounds should signify meanings at all does not seem necessary; and the fact that an articulate word is *understood* to have a definite meaning shows the arbitrariness of human speech. Thus also the written word 'distance' is wholly unlike the uttered sound or the visual colors which also serve to suggest distance, or finally the tactual or muscular data which likewise introduce the idea of distance into the mind. Neither is there any necessary connection between colors and tangible magnitude. "Confusion [in the outlines of the object] or faintness [of color] have no more a necessary connection with little or great magnitude than they have with little or great distance."[2] "Farther, when one has by experience learned the connection there is between the several ideas of sight and touch, he will be able, by the perception he has of the situation of visible things in respect of one another, to make a sudden and true estimate of the situation of outward, tangible things corresponding to them. And thus he shall perceive *by sight* the situation of external objects, which do not properly fall under that sense.[3]"

With regard to the nature of this connection, "when, upon perception of an idea, I range it under this or that sort it is because it is perceived after the same manner, or because it has a likeness or conformity with or affects me in the same way as the ideas of the sort I rank it under"[4] Thus the experience of a customary connection between ideas is sufficient to account for the presence of the phenomenal object, and the manner in which this connection is brought about is by our perceiving the likeness

---

[1] 'Philosophy of Berkeley' in "Life, Letters, etc.," pp. 374-375. Fraser; "Berkeley," Blackwood Series, p. 198.

[2] "Theory of Vision," § 58.

[3] Ibid § 99.

[4] Ibid § 128.

or conformity of one idea with another or recognizing that we are affected by one idea as we are affected by another. The arbitrariness of human language is paralleled by this arbitrariness of the sense symbolism, and in both cases it is experience that instructs us in the use of these symbols. The externalization of objects in space Berkeley takes to be accounted for by his sensationalistic machinery; and Space, in any other sense than as an empirical product, here falls under the general condemnation of abstract ideas.[1] So likewise Time is the empirical succession of sensations, not, as with Locke, a succession taken to denote time, but a succession constitutive of time.

In § 147 of the Theory of Vision the empirical theory as it appears to Berkeley is fairly summed up. It is as follows: "Upon the whole, I think we may fairly conclude that the proper objects of vision constitute the Universal Language of Nature, whereby we are instructed how to regulate our actions, in order to attain those things that are necessary to the preservation and well being of our bodies, as also to avoid whatever may be hurtful and destructive of them. It is by this information that we are principally guided in all the transactions and concerns of life. And the manner wherein they signify and mark out unto us the objects which are at a distance is the same with that of languages and signs of human appointment; which do not suggest the things signified by any likeness or identity of nature, but only by an *habitual* connection that experience has made us to observe between them."[2] This constitutes Berkely's empiricism, "a position which was never lost sight of in spite of later rationalistic developments; for, twenty-three years after the Theory of Vision was published, its vindication appeared, in which is maintained the governing principle of that former work, viz. the passivity of all ideas in so far as they are received as mere particulars, regardless of the combining and relating activity" of mind.

But we may ask: does this perceived likeness between ideas mean merely a way that sensations have of forming themselves into groups, and so constituting a product utterly unlike the sensations of which it is composed; or, since sensations are in themselves heterogeneous, is there implied in the perceived likeness a reference to the combining activity of mind? Now Berkeley makes no enquiry into the presuppositions which render experience possible; he does not search out principles or categories which function in a manifold of sense foreign to them by nature. Unitary mind, as active, synthetic, is the presupposition from which he starts. His dualism is not between sense and under-

---

[1] Fraser; "Berkeley," Blackwood Philos. Classics, p. 136.
[2] Theory of Vision, § 147.

standing; it is between mind and mind. By reference to mind as the conscious unity of a manifold, Locke's primary qualities had been reduced to their condition of mind-dependence, and in Berkeley's empirical explanation of the constitution of the object, sensations are regarded as significant signs only because of their relation to mind. This is apparent even in the "Theory of Vision," and, if one reads his earlier philosophy in the light of his later work, it seems less necessary to read Berkeley through Hume. That mind or self was at first conceived by means of crude categories, and thus justly merited the censure of Hume, it would be idle to dispute; but the spirit-substance was only a feeble echo of Locke's *tabula rasa* and foreign to Berkeley's 'active mind' and to the 'Reason' of "Siris."

b. Necessary Connection.

We have already noticed that the ideas of sense are distinguished from those of imagination, first, because of their greater liveliness and distinctness; second, because of their independence of the individual mind; finally, from the observed fact of their appearing in a regular, orderly and coherent series. It was reserved for Hume to give exclusive prominence to the first of these distinctions; but for Berkeley this liveliness and distinctness of the ideas of sense is merely a characteristic mark observed to accompany ideas whose special designating feature is the orderliness and regularity of their production.

The phenomenal object having been resolved into its sensational constituents, no likeness or affinity between these sensations or objects of the special senses can be discovered. No value attaches to them except as they are understood to be signs and so recognized by the mind by reference to which their meanings are exhibited in the gradual unfolding of experience. Experience "teaches us that such and such ideas are attended with such and such other ideas "[1]—herein consists the arbitrariness of the connection—but "the set rules or established methods wherein the Mind we depend on excites in us the ideas of sense, are called the laws of nature; and these we learn by experience."[2] And "all this we know, not by discovering any necessary connection between our ideas, but only by the observation of the settled laws of nature."[3] The law of cause and effect does not subsist between ideas, for these, as mere passive particulars, serve only as signs by which the mind is enabled to gather rational meanings and understand the laws imposed upon the finite by a Supreme Mind; for ideas of sense, being impressed in accordance with "Rules or Laws of

---

[1] "Principles"; § 30.
[2] Ibid.
[3] Ibid §31.

Nature, speak themselves the effects of a mind more powerful and wise than human spirits."[1] Thus no phenomenal object can be a cause, phenomena are merely effects, and, in the case of an apparent affinity of one substance for another or the observed attraction of one body to another, nothing is *signified* besides the effect itself.

To the objection that for purposes of scientific enquiry secondary causes, at least, must be admitted, Berkeley replies that the hypothesis of the uniformity and invariability of nature is in no wise affected upon his principles. "There are certain general laws that run through the whole chain of natural effects; these are learned by the observation and study of nature, and are by men applied . . to the explaining of the various phenomena—which explanation consists only in showing the conformity any particular phenomenon hath to the general laws of nature, or, which is the same thing, in discovering the uniformity there is in the production of natural effects."[2] Complete knowledge of the phenomenon we cannot have, not because it is in its nature alien to mind, but because the 'efficient cause' which produces it is the 'will of a spirit'; yet we can obtain "a greater largeness of comprehension, whereby analogies, harmonies and agreements are discovered in the works of nature, and the particular effects explained, that is, reduced to general rules"[3]—or categories.

In the Principles of Human Knowledge the objectivity of the laws, by means of which a world in space and time is made possible, is seemingly accepted as a fact based upon simple observation of phenomena, than which there are no more ultimate facts for us. In the unitariness of the phenomenon we have not only a thing as a cluster of sensations marked by one name, but a thing which in its unity is itself an object of consciousness, an idea. Accordingly, as we have elsewhere said, the character of the phenomenon is not completely exhausted in the mere discovery of its sensational constituents, for simple observation of it, as it is intuitively apprehended in consciousness, reveals it a thing, distinguished from other things, in spite of psychological analysis and the mere description of how it has come to be. But not being independent of mind, the further explication of phenomena must again take place only with reference to mind; i. e., I must simply observe the relation between mind and phenomena in this second character. This reveals that phenomena, as also the relations which apparently subsist between them, are independent of *my* mind, i. e., mind in so far as I have a knowledge of its acts and operations; and this constitutes, in Berkeley's earlier philosophy, the objectivity of natural phenomena and the laws by which they are governed.

---

[1] "Principles"; § 36.
[2] Ibid § 62.
[3] Ibid § 105.

Thus, (1) the 'Principles' endeavors to establish the objectivity of laws upon the the observation of ideas as ultimate facts of consciousness, which presumably reveals the fact that these phenomena and their relations are independent of the indiviual will. (2) Accordingly they are to be referred to a Supreme Mind here conceived under the catagory of Will. From this there results a subordination of Reason to Will and the apparent liability of these objective laws of nature (even granting their objectivity to have been established by so simple a process) to be subverted by a capricious Will;—"we may discover the general laws of nature, and from them deduce the other phenomena; I do not say demonstate, for all deduction of that kind depends on a supposition that the Author of Nature always operates uniformily, and in constant observance of those rules we take for principles—which we cannot evidently know."[1]

It is in the 'Principles' that the sufficiency of the Berkeleian sign language for the explanation of experience seems most apparently to depend upon the support of a deistic theology, while, in Siris, Reason rather than Will is looked upon as the supreme category; and the discovery of the objectivity of law is based upon a deeper insight into the implications of the phenomenal objects, and a recognition of the inadequacy of the early empirical position as an ultimate explanation of the phenomenal universe. "The inner bonds which weld the perceived universe into a rational whole are now made subjects of reflection,[2] and the issue is the discovery that the universals of Reasons are immanent in sense. In accordance with the established connections, no longer referred to the arbitrary imposition of Divine Will, it is seen that "the mind of man acts by an instrument necessarily. The τὸ ἡγεμονιχὸν, or mind presiding in the world acts by an instrument freely.[3] Secondary causes are now admitted; for "without instrumental and secondary causes, there could be no regular course of nature. And without a regular course nature could never be understood."[4] Berkeley never dreams of departing from his early belief that mechanical causes cannot be received as ultimate explanations; but there is a much stronger insistence upon their usefulness and necessity, as mechanical hypotheses. "There is an *analogy, constancy* and *uniformity* in the phenomena or appearances of nature, which are a foundation for general rules; and these are a Grammar for the understanding of Nature"[5] and "so far as men have studied and remarked its rules, and can

---

[1] Ibid §107. Works Vol. I.
[2] Wenley; "British Thought and Modern Speculation"; in Scottish Review, Jan., 1892, vol. 19, p. 150.
[3] "Siris" § 160.
[4] "Siris" § 160.
[5] "Siris" § 252.

interpret right, so far they may be said to be knowing in nature."[1] We must now clearly recognize that sense is of itself insufficient to constitute the phenomenal world of objects as we find it. The phenomena of nature strike on the senses and are *understood* by the mind[2] i. e., 'Thought, Reason, Intellect, introduce us into the knowledge of their causes.'[3] Again, it is certain that the "principles of science are neither objects of Sense or imagination;"[4] "Science consists not in the passive perceptions but in the reasoning upon them."[5]

Thus we are brought in Siris to the knowledge of a new world in which "such is the mutual relation, connection, motion and sympathy of the parts that they seem, as it were, animated and held together by one soul; and such is their harmony, order, and regular course, as sheweth the soul to be governed and directed by a Mind."[6]

As we are now constrained to interpret Berkeley's Language of Nature, we find that we must no longer read it as a system of signs, arbitrarily instituted by capricious Will, but as signs whose sole value is in their rational significance. In the new universe, with which we are now made acquainted, the continuity remains unbroken. From the lowest sense given phenomena we ascend in a series of gradations to the highest products of Reason by means of which are discovered the inviolable laws immanent in an objective system of nature. True, the various steps by which this unfolding of nature is accomplished are frequently dominated by the hylozoistic and animistic conceptions of the past. Accordingly no philosophy of nature, worthy the name, is offered us, nor indeed is such seriously intended by Berkeley in his review of the antiquated categories of past philosophies; but the central feature which serves to differentiate his later from his earlier idealism nevertheless remains. The world is now to be viewed as an organic whole, whose several parts are throughout concatenated and sustained by one Mind. Exeept for the important fact that Mind is now conceived as Reason immanent in the world rather than as dominant Will, the new conceptions do not seem so foreign to his former idealism; yet by this there is apparently introduced a world-wide distinction between his later and earlier doctrines.

If we attempt to discover the source of these new conceptions we come upon a nowise unfamiliar assertion that 'the Mind, her acts and faculties, furnish a new and distinct class of objects,'[7] and

---

[1] "Siris," § 254.
[2] Ibid.
[3] Ibid § 268.
[4] Ibid.
[5] Ibid § 305.
[6] Ibid § 273.
[7] Ibid § 297.

these 'objects' are what Berkeley variously denominates 'Ideas,' intellectual "ideas," intellectual "notions," and 'notions.' Now the
thorough recognition of the *immanence* of Reason in the Berkelian
world of phenomena forbids our believing that he has espoused the
cause of Platonism with the ardor of a complete devotee. Siris,
indeed, is thoroughly imbued with the spirit of Plato; but to Plato,
Berkeley has never been a complete stranger, either to his spirit.or
in the knowledge of his works. The passages suggestive of Plato,
and in some instances quoted from him, Berkeley turns to account
in showing a 'closer correlation of sense and intellect' than the
former achieves, while at the same time the passivity of the idea
through which Berkeley reached his early empiricism is not abandoned.[1] The following indicate his more explicit recognition in
"Siris" of the several functions that may be assigned to mind it its
diverse operations.

In the first place "Sense implies an impression from some
other being, and denotes a dependence in the soul which hath
it,"[2] a statement clearly recalling the influence of Locke and indeed not unsuggestive of Kant, if one bears in mind that the ding-
an-sich must somehow be conceptualized, or else—an alternative of
course adopted by Fichte and the Hegelians—it declares itself to
be nothing. Again:—"By experiments of sense we become acquainted with the lower faculties of the soul; from them, whether
by a gradual evolution or ascent, we arrive at the highest. Sense
supplies images to memory. These become subjects for fancy to
work upon. Reason considers and judges of the imaginations.
And these acts of reason become new *objects* of the understanding.'[3] Further to illustrate the small part that is played by mere
sense, apart from the active functioning of Reason:—"as understanding perceiveth not, thất is, doth not hear, or see, or feel" [as
do the special senses], "so sense knoweth not . . . . . sense or
soul, *so far forth as sensitive*, knoweth nothing."[4] And now if we
would know what this has to do with the phenomenal object, we
may note that "we know a thing when we understand it; and we
understand it when we can interpret or tell what it signifies. . . . .
We perceive, indeed, sounds by hearing, and characters by sight.
But we are not therefore said to understand them."[5] They are

---

[1] Berkeley's 'notions' are Locke's ideas of relation and by them "he proposes to effect a compromise between the *tabula rasa* of Aristotle and the *innate
ideas* of Plato and suggests that though "there are properly no ideas or passive
objects but what were derived from Sense," yet there are also, besides these, "her
own acts and operations [acts of the mind], such as notions,' which must be
referable to the understanding, ... here Berkeley clearly approximates
to Kant." T. H. Webb; "Veil of Isis," p. 27.

[2] "Siris," § 286.

[3] Ibid § 303.

[4] Ibid § 305.

[5] Ibid § 253.

unintelligible save as they are subjected to the unifying acts of Reason. In the uncategorized sense impressions there is only unintelligible sound, unintelligible color, 'perceived' or 'rather present to sense, but not understood, not truly perceived or apperceived. Only the correlate of sensations into which unity is introduced by the mind is truly regarded as an object distinguished from other objects and related to them. The former individualized percept is now looked at from the point of view of its other implications, and there is seen to be involved in its being the informing principle of active, unitary mind.[1]

We may now ask whether this later Rationalism is at variance with Berkeley's early idealism, or whether it merely represents the greater elaboration of elements already contained in the philosophy of the "Principles of Human Knowledge." Accordingly, let us retrace our steps, delaying for a moment at the fourth of the seven dialogues entitled "Alciphron, or the Minute Philosopher." The series of arguments here put forth are in the nature of rational inferences from the various sensations with which we are affected, purporting to discover to us that the 'Optic Language' we before considered solely from the point of view of the arbitrariness of signs regarded in themselves "hath a necessary connexion with knowledge wisdom and goodness." By rational inferences from the acts, gestures, and speech of our fellowmen we are enabled to conclude the existence of other selves conceived in analogy with our own. By parity of reasoning the sign language of Nature viewed in its totality is significant of a Mind upon whom Nature is constantly dependent for its existence, a design argument being supported in maintenance of a theistic view. Here we are told, in anticipation of Siris, that every perception of an object involves the work of rational inference. The mere signs or sensations which, like the printed words of a page, are, in their own Nature of small moment, carry the attention onward to the very things signified . . . . which in truth and strictness are not seen, but only suggested and apprehended" *by means of* the proper objects of sight. We have, again, the doctrine of the Theory of Vision, with a greater insistence, not only upon the insignificance of sensations regarded in themselves, but also a more explicit recognition of the function of mind in *apprehending* the object. Likewise the cus-

---

[1] 'No sooner does intellect dawn upon the shadowy scene, 'than we perceive the true principle of unity, identity and existence.' Those things which before seemed to constitute the whole of being, upon taking an intellectual view of things [i. e., viewing them as conceptions] prove to be but fleeing phantoms.'
In presence of such declarations, Professor Fraser declares that Berkeley ' not only was not a sensualist of the school of Condillac, not only not an empiricist of the school of Hume, but he was a transcendentalist of the highest and purest school of Kant . . . . . ' Cf. also Lewis: "The History of Philosophy from Thales to Comte," vol. II, pp. 304, 305.

tom-induced association between sensations takes on a different coloring now from that observable in the Theory of Vision, and we are told that "there must be time and experience, by repeated acts, to acquire *a habit of knowing* the connexion between the signs and the things signified." [1] This seems in essential agreement with a passage in Siris[2] which states that "mind, knowledge and notions, either in habit or in act, always go together." That habit which is unconsciously rational is the basis of our immediate perceptions of the phenomenal object, is the view which Berkeley adopts in "Alciphron" and later urges in his doctrine of the immanence of Reason in the world of sense.

Here we must pause for the moment, since it is plain that the negative theory of the "Principles" and the dialogues between Hylas and Philonous, repeating with slight variations the former doctrine, can offer but feeble suggestion of the rationalism which creeps into "Siris" through the dialogue we have briefly noticed. There thus arises the question of whether "Alciphron" and "Siris" should not be, together, regarded as representative of Berkeley's later thought, while the "Theory of Vision," the "Principles" and the earlier dialogues remain to vindicate a view of the world between which and the later idealism there is little or no connection. The lines upon which we must seek an answer to this question are suggested by the further inquiry that naturally arises from the preceeding, viz.: how, in a Philosophy which preached Nominalism at the outset, have we any right to speak of rational connections and the dominance of mind in a universe in which by hypothesis our knowledge is confined to particulars. Accordingly we can expect to find essential agreement between these two seemingly opposed types of philosophy only in the discovery that the conceptual processes implied in Berkeley's later theory of the constitution of experience are not at variance with the earlier. That the mind and its acts make us aware of an entirely different class of objects from the mere sense ideas, we are told in "Siris"; and this is but a repetition of § 89[3] of the "Principles" in which we learn that we have a *notion* of relations between things or ideas—which relations are distinct from the ideas or things related, inasmuch as the latter may be perceived by us without our perceiving the former. In other words, the mind by its acts *conceives* the relations between things, while these latter may be viewed as mere particulars apart from the rational implications that are throughout contained in the constitution of the object. Thus from the consideration of relations between ideas, which has so far in this chapter occupied our attention, we

---

[1] Fraser; "Selections from Berkeley," p. 269.
[2] "Siris," § 309.
[3] Cf., p. 13—note.

must now turn to the 'notion' by means of which we obtain our knowledge of relations.

2. THE NOTION AND ITS OBJECTS.

(a). *Meaning of 'Notion.'*

In the section on abstract ideas we endeavored to set forth Berkeley's distinction between ideas in the sense of abstract images, and in that of representative notions. All ideas, which are, in one aspect, particular,—herein consists his Nominalism—are in another aspect representative of other particulars,—and in this consists his Rationalism. They are alike abstractions from the phenomenal object. In one aspect we see that they are translatable into terms of mind as percipient, in the other into terms of mind as cognitive. In any case, the existence of the object involves a reference to mind, not only as merely percipient, but as cognitive.

In Berkeley's early idealism we have seen that it is the relation of the phenomenal object to *percipient* consciousness that is chiefly insisted upon. The percept is individualized, resolved into its constituent factors by means of its discoverable relation to con-sciousness in so far as the latter denotes a passive experience—percipience. At this stage we note the arbitrariness of the relation between phenomena thus particularized. Why this particular atomic element of consciousness should be connected with that other particular, passive experience, does not appear.[1] The reason of the connection, if any there be, has been lost in the past experience of the individual or the race, in the course of which such facility has been gained in interpretation of this Universal Sign Language that the necessity of its origin and maintenance in Universal Mind is neglected. The sensations, which have no bond in themselves, since they serve only as signs, must have a causal source or ground in which the reason of their connection can be found, a source that is independent of the individual will, and in which, as we finally learn in "Siris," we can only participate by means of the universals of Reason.

In the "Principles of Human Knowledge," Berkeley recognized the existence of these universals; for, as Mr. Bradley[2] has said, he knew that "Relation constitutes the universality of ideas." Hence "his third kind of existence, the knowledge of which is given us by a notion." But, as the same author further says, Berkeley does not follow up the 'notion' "because blinded by the ambiguity of the idea derived from Locke." Abstract ideas Berkeley indeed denies, —though only, as we have said, in the sense of abstract images—

---

[1] Berkeley—Fraser (Blackwood Series), p. 198.
[2] C. W. Bradley; "Berkeley's Idealism," in Journal of Speculative Philos. 1881–82.

for every idea has its particular aspect; but the phenomenal object likewise retains its conceptual character; it is related to other things, and is one of an organic whole whose several parts are interdependent and ultimately imply a rational nexus. That the unifying bond between phenomena, implied in the recognition of their causal source, is not suggested in the " Principles " otherwise than in his brief acknowledgement of 'relations,' is true; but it would be false to assert that Berkeley had no basis for his future rationalizing, and that he reached his later philosophy by means of the abstractions which he had at first denied. Nor is this so inconsistent with a statement occurring early in the "Principles" and which seems to curtail our knowledge: "my conceiving or imagining power", he there tells us, "does not extend beyond the possibility of real existence." For, as we have endeavored to show, by real existence Berkeley never means the mere object of the special senses, but the percept;[1] and the doctrine of "Alciphron," that "every perception implies more than it *preceptively* intimates,"[2] is but the development of a view for which he was already prepared in the recognition of the representative character belonging to all perception.

To repeat in brief Berkeley's theory respecting universals, the percept, or phenomenal object, immediately present to consciousness is, in so far as it can be referred to individual conscious experience, resolvable into particulars. Accordingly, the percept is itself particular, and likewise all general notions or concepts are particular, since by reference to the immediate perceptual character of the individual consciousness their composite nature is discovered. "But two things which God has joined together cannot be put asunder without loss to both," and if we cannot, from the foregoing, abstract the object from sensation and ascribe to it an existence independent of conscious experience, neither can we hypostatize mere sensations and give to them an ultimate reality which we deny to the objective consciousness involved in the immediate perception of things.

From the third dialogue between Hylas and Philonous it may be seen that a possible Humian hypostatization of sensations was present to Berkeley's mind; and he seems there struggling to free his conception of the self from the crude categories in which it appears clothed in the Principles, a task which he better achieved in Siris. But it never appeared to him that he would himself be regarded as a representative of sensationalism, and that, in exhibiting the necessary relation of all objects to the percipient con-

---

[1] Philosophy of Berkeley in "The Life, Letters and Unpublished Writings of Berkeley," p. 371–372.

[2] Werley; "British Thought and Modern Speculation," in Scottish Rev., Vol. 19, p. 140.

sciousness, he had debarred himself from any further consideration of those universals of Reason, upon the assumed existence of which the whole of his later theory reposes. To hypostatize universals or notions, in other words, to conceive an 'abstract idea' that cannot be shown to bear the marks which signify its origination in individual experience, is an impossibility. While on the other hand, to hypostatize sensations, to regard them as having an existence independent of the relating activity of mind, is again to commit that fallacy of abstractly conceiving existence to which it was Berkeley's purpose to call attention. That particular sensations are of themselves insufficient for the ultimate explanation of our experience of an objective world, Berkeley acknowledges in the admission that "all knowledge and demonstration are about universal notions." Things which, regarded in themselves, and as mere passive objects of mind, are particular, become universal by being regarded in their relation to mind from which they cannot ultimately be separated.

In the second edition of the Principles[1] we are told that there subsist relations between things and that these relations are discoverable by means of the 'notion.' The notion, we are also told in the first edition, is the particular in its representative character, not as representative of anything beyond and distinct from consciousness, but representative of other particulars whose sole significance is their relation to conscious mind. Accordingly, the Berkelian notion is a representative image,[2] the obverse of the particular whose constituent elements are discoverable by psychological analysis; but this representative or conceptual[3] character is as much a given

---

[1] The fact that this statement occurs only in the second edition of the Principles has been cited as proof positive, not only that in the earliest phase of his idealism Berkeley had but imperfectly conceived the function of the intellectual notion, a fact readily to be conceded; but it has also been held to denote a more fundamental difference, such that the earlier and later theories could not have been held together in solution by Berkeley. Such objections do not however sufficiently explain the fact that in the second edition of the Principles, published in 1732, so shortly before the appearance of Siris, the empiricism of the first edition reappears in substantially the same form that it assumes in the earlier. Cf. McCosh; "Locke's Theory of Knowledge with a notice of Berkeley" in "Criteria of Truth."

[2] Representative of *conscious experience*, not of a reality independent of all consciousness tor, as Lewes says: "Nothing can be more inaccurate than to class Berkeley among those who maintain ideas to be representative of things: ideas he says are things. Yet Hamilton commits this inaccuracy."—History of Philo., Vol. II, p. 313, note.

[3] i. e., The concept must be individualized. "Yet this rule," says Mansel, ('Proleg. Logica,' pp. 23, 33, quoted by Fraser in 'Selections,' page 21, note 2)," *individualize your concepts* does not mean sensationalize them. With Berkeley, however, as we have seen, it does mean sensationalize them, although this does not exclude the representative character of the concept. For: "a blurred picture is just as much a single mental fact as a sharp picture is; and *the use of either picture*

fact of consciousness as the particular image which in one aspect it is seen to be. The particular only exists with reference to the universal, while, on the other hand, the universal has no abstract existence apart from the particular. For this reason Professor Fraser's contention that Berkeley makes ideas objective, rather than things subjective, seems to be borne out even in the earlier theory. " I am not for changing things into ideas, bat rather ideas into things," says Berkeley; "since those immediate objects of perception, which, according to you, are only appearances of things, I take to be the real things themselves "

Judging from his early statements with regard to the notion, and from the subsequent part which they play in his later idealism, it does not seem that such statements of the realistic position he wished to defend should be taken merely as an attempt to square a subjective idealism with the common sense conviction that there is an external world which is for its existence independent of the individual consciousness. For Berkeley, the objectivity of ideas and relations between ideas was guaranteed, (1) by throughout maintaining that, in showing the subjective reference which any phenomenon has, he is not thereby destroying the independent

---

by the mind to symbolize a whole class of individuals is a new mental function." (James: "Psych.," vol. II, p 49). In other words: the "Mind, her acts and faculties, furnish a new and distinct class of objects," (cited above, "Siris," § 247) or ' notions,' and the notion is just this ' blurred picture,' not in its character as re solvable into its constituents in the individual consciousness, but in the *use which the mind makes of it.* To quote from an article of recent date, (Dr. A. K. Rogers' "Epistemology and Experience:" Philos. Rev., Sept., 1898). "The concept has existence only as a tool, a method. It is not any element of experience as an existence, but simply the way we use that particular element which we call the image. Accordingly, the concept, the universal as such does not enter into reality at all except in its functional use. It is quite impossible that anything should exist in general."

Now I think Berkeley would say, this functional use of the concept in experience must be justified, and we find its justification in the representative image; for, in the latter, this functional use of the concept, this reference beyond the mere particulars of which the representative image is composed is a given fact of experience. The dynamic representative character of the concept or ' notion,' the reference forward to other reality than itself, is as much a fact, seized and transfixed, and thus justified in experience, as its static character—which is its natural history and the description of its particular, constituent, psychic factors—and experience cannot be other than it takes itself to be.

The representative ' image or notion' is thus a go-between in two phases of our attitude toward reality. *As representative* it is functionally active as the concept; as static, passive, translatable into terms of the individual consciousness, it is composite and thus resolvable into particulars. *As concept* it is ideally predicable in the judgment but this predication, though ideal, finds its justification in the fact that the sense datum which forms the subject of judgment is also ideal and in the unitariness of the representative image are the two made one.

Thus, beneath the surface contradiction which appears in many parts of Berkeley's philosophy the divergent lines of Siris and the Principles meet in a common focus—the doctrine of the ' notion.'

character of the object, since objectivity is a given fudamental fact of consciousness; (2) by the preseace in consciousness of universals or 'notions.' In denying the existence of abstract notions,[2] i. e., in the discovery that the notion always involves a relation to sense perception Berkeley had vindicated the reality of the notion and thus the objectivity of the relations which form its content by the direct evidence of the perceptual consciousness. For the content of the notion is, he tell us, relations, relations which at any rate *appear* objective, and since the notion is, in its individual character, as the image, *experiential*, the objectivity of relations is directly evinced by consciousness; for—to use Professor Royce's language--experience cannot be other than it takes itself to be. In other words, Berkeley asserts a common sense realism,[2] resting the existence of universals upon the direct testimony of consciousness. His realism is not, however, a copy theory, for there is nothing foreign to consciousness of which the idea can be the copy, and in this respect it is idealism.

In the third dialogue between Hylas and Phylonous, the notion in the guise of the archetype plays a more prominent part than in the "Principles," and likewise the objectivity of ideas is further insisted upon. While in the later work we find Berkeley denying the existence of abstract matter, for the reason that the existence of a thing cannot be abstracted from the perception of it, we here find him using the same argument in support of the objectivity of things or ideas to mind, for "that a thing should be really perceived by my consciousness and at the same time not really exist is to me a plain contradiction, since I cannot prescind or abstract, even in thought, the existence of a sensible thing from its being perceived."

In "Siris" we receive further insight into the doctrine of the objectivity of ideas, which, from his now complete recognition of the immanence of reason, one would expect to find him regard as active in their objective aspect. And so it is, for he there says that sensible qualities are to be regarded as acts only in the *cause*, and as passions in *us*. In Siris also[3] Berkeley favors a doctrine of 'innate notions,' although, as he tells us, it is different from that which is favored by the moderns, doubtless meaning the abstract idea of Locke as well as the innate idea of Descartes. For the 'innate notion' Berkeley describes as having a potential existence:

---

[1] It is the emptiness of the abstract universal as well as its unimaginableness against which Berkeley declaims—the unschematized category. But Berkeley had no dualism as had Kant—no violent severing of sense-given impressions from the activity of thought.

[2] Cf. Wenley—British Thought and Modern Speculation, p. 148 of Scottish Rev., vol. 19.

[3] Siris § 308-309-315.

it is connate rather than innate. The finite mind or self, by participation in the Divine Mind, possesses the power of reflection and of originating its own products, the notions; but since this reflection is employed upon sense phenomena, which are not by nature foreign to Mind, the notion amounts to an active synthesis of this given material, and is thus for Berkeley *constitutive*, or to express it more nearly in Berkeley's Platonic language, by means of the notion we rediscover the universal creative 'form' of the Divine Reason immanent in sense.

(*b*)   *Notion of Self and God.*

Parallel to Berkeley's theory of a notion of relations there also develops his 'notion' of the Self and God. With regard to our knowledge of Self it is again Locke who furnishes a point of departure for Berkeley's theory. The former, in close imitation of Descartes, had said[1] that "as for our own existence we perceive it so plainly, that it neither needs nor is capable of any proof. For nothing can be more evident to us than our own existence. . . . . Experience convinces us that we can have an *intuitive knowledge* of our own existence, and an internal infallible perception that we are. In every act of sensation, reasoning, or thinking we are conscious to ourselves of our own being; and in this matter come not short of the highest degree of certainty."

Apparently in entire agreement with this, Berkeley sets out with a intuitional view of the self. Such passages as the following appear in considerable profusion throughout his earlier philosophical works, and demonstrate his inability to free himself from an apparent necessity of giving to his conception of the self an empirical setting. In the "Principles" he says that "we comprehend our own existence by inward *feeling or reflection*, and that of other spirits by reason."[2]   Likewise, in the third dialogue between Hylas and Philonous: "I do nevertheless know that I who am a spirit or thinking substance, exist as certainly as I know my ideas exist. Further, I know what I mean by the terms I and myself, and I know this *immediately* or *intuitively*, though I do not perceive it as I perceive a triangle, a color, or a sound." By such statements Berkeley not only laid himself open to the charge of having attempted to ground his metaphysic upon a psychological theory of the self—a view which a consistent application of his own empirical principles would destroy; for, as Hume afterward showed, the permanence of the I, as given in perception, is not a real permanence—but he apparently sought to reinstate, notwithstanding his

---

[1] Locke's Essay, Book IV, ch. ix–3.
[2] "Principles," § 89.

Nominalism, a 'substance' theory fully as unacceptable as that of Locke.

Early in the Principles this category of substance appears; yet it occurs rather as a foil to the Cartesian substance than as a principle of explanation to which the author attached any positive significance —a category nearest at hand to envisage the active principle which, by the extension of its activity, was to supplant passive matter. We have no mediaeval discussion of faculties, no question is raised as to the relation of a soul substance to a divine spirit substance, nor are we told anything about the attributes of this substance. On the contrary--in speaking of the perception of the qualities of bodies— he says that these qualities are in the mind only as they are perceived by it—that is, *not by way of mode or attribute*, but only by way of 'idea.' Following the passage just quoted, Berkeley proceeds to draw the conclusion that the soul does not possess 'qualities.' Subject, mode, and attribute, of the philosophers are discarded as unintelligible terms; and this he illustrates in the case of a material object.[1]

The paralogism involved in the attempt to explain the self by means of the materialistic category of substance certainly appeared to Berkeley. In the first place they would, of necessity, occur to him in the distinction which he set up between spirits and ideas. The latter, as merely passive existences, have nothing in common with spirit but the general name Being. This distinction is introduced among the reflections of the Commonplace Book: "Things are two fold," he tells us—"active or inactive." The existence of active things is to act, of inactive to be 'perceived.' There being nothing in common between these two heterogeneous kinds of existences, the former, the active relational principle, mind or spirit, cannot be adequately expressed in terms of passive ideas. Accordingly, in spite of a seemingly bold assertion that 'we assuredly have an idea of substance,' we read its qualification in the statements which follow: "The substance of body we know. The substance of Spirit we do not know—it not being knowable, it being a *purus actus.*"

Now by the 'substance of body,' Berkeley, as we have seen, means nothing else than the sensible object, involving indeed thought-relations if we read him aright, but never abstract substance. Likewise any knowledge of spirit *as substance* is here denied.

In the Principles and in the earlier dialogues, the category of substance occurs in connection with his various other characterizations of mind or spirit. In the third of these dialogues,[2] after speaking of the 'I as a spirit' or 'thinking substance,' he goes on

[1] "Principles," § 49.
[2] "Philonous" 3d dialogue, § 5.

to say: "The Mind, Spirit or Soul, is that indivisible, unextended thing which thinks, acts, and perceives. I say indivisable, *because unextended*; and unextended *because extended, figured, moveable things are ideas;*" and that which perceives ideas, which thinks and wills, is plainly itself no idea, nor like an idea . . . . I·do not therefore say my soul is an idea, or like an idea." These statements do not seem to be a return to scholastic discussions as to the possible existence of a spirit substance, stripped of all the relations by which substance or matter is perceptively known· to us. They appear rather to indicate the predominant thought in Berkeley's mind, that neither the sense qualities nor substance which exists only in presence of these qualities can be adduced in support of a kind of existence which is, in itself, unknowable. Only a negative signification is assigned to substance;[1] and Berkeley, whenever he is driven to an explanation of the self or the objective Spirit which for him takes the place of matter, has recourse to the 'active, thinking principle,' a knowledge of which is had by means of the notion.

After denying the possibility of our having an idea either of the self or of God, he proceeds to give a reason for his insistence that we have, if not an idea, at least some knowledge, of Spirit. In reply to Hylas' objection that even if abstract matter be disallowed, there may yet be "some third nature distinct from Matter and Spirit"—"for what reason is there why you should call it Spirit"?—Berkeley in effect says that there can be no *via media* between matter and spirit, no *unica substantia*[2] for as "I have a mind to have some notion of meaning in what I say . . . when I speak of an active being, I am obliged to mean spirit." Activity can be ascribed only to that which has ideas and possesses the power of 'combining and relating' those ideas, or to that which creates ideas.

If I may be allowed to quote farther, at considerable length, from the dialogue we have been considering, the following may be taken as illustrative of the position at which Berkeley has thus far arrived with regard to a knowledge of the self and God. Though we have no idea of spirit, yet "taking the word idea in a large sense, my soul may be said to furnish me with an idea [notion], that is, an *image* or likeness of God—though indeed extremely inadequate. For all the notion I have of God is obtained by reflecting on my own soul, heightening its powers, and removing its imperfection."[3] In this we seem to obtain some hint of Berkeley's

---

[1] Lewis, in his History of Philosophy (Berkeley) holds to the extreme of this substance-interpretation of Berkeley. He tells us that his "idealism is at bottom the much decried system of Spinoza, who taught that there was but one essence in the universe, and that one Substance."

[2] cf. Fraser; Berkeley, Blackwood Philos. Classics, p. 201.

[3] Third dialogue between Hylas and Philonous. Wales—Vol.

later doctrine of Personality, God appearing to be for him the completion of the finite self. He further describes this sort of knowledge in the following terms: "I have, therefore, though not an inactive idea, yet in *myself* some sort of an active thinking *image* of the Deity. And though I perceive Him not by sense, yet I have a *notion* of him, or know him by reflection and reasoning."[1]

To this statement of Philonous, Hylas, the materialist, objects. "You say," he remarks, "your own soul supplies you with some sort of an idea or image of God. But, at the same time, you acknowledge you have, properly speaking, no *idea* of your own soul. . . . To act consistently, you must either admit Matter or reject Spirit." "Philonous thus replies, "I say, in the first place, that I do not deny the existence of material substance, merely because I have no notion of it, but because the notion of it is inconsistent; or, in other words, because it is repugnant that there should be a notion of it. Many things, for ought I know, may exist, whereof neither I nor any other man hath or can have any idea or notion whatsoever. But then those things must be possible, that is, nothing inconsistent must be included in their definition. I say, secondly, that although we believe things to exist which we do not perceive, yet we may not believe that any particular thing exists, without some reason for such belief; but I have no reason for believing the existence of matter. I have no immediate intuition thereof: neither can I immediately from my sensations, ideas, notions, actions, or passions, infer an unthinking, unperceiving, inactive Substance— either by probable deduction or necessary consequence. Whereas the being of my *Self*, that is, my own soul, mind, or thinking principle, I evidently know *by reflection.* . . . . It is granted we have neither an immediate evidence nor a demonstrative knowledge of the existence of other finite spirits; but it will not thence follow that such spirits are on a foot with material substances: if to suppose the one be inconsistent, and it be not inconsistent to suppose the other; if the one can be inferred by no argument, and there is a probability for the other. . . . I say, lastly, that I have a notion of Spirit, though I have not, strictly speaking, an idea of it. I do not perceive it as an idea, or by means of an idea, but know it *by reflection.*"

In the above we have not only Berkeley's second and positive disproof of abstract matter—the first and negative disproof being grounded on the fact that its existence is not supported by the evidence of immediate perception—but, what is here to our purpose, his reasons for substituting spirit for abstract matter.

We may put the case briefly thus: We can have no idea of

---

[1] "Third Dialogue between Hylas and Philonous."

spirit, but only a notion or conception of it. We have neither an idea of abstract matter nor can we conceive its existence. The notion of matter is self-contradictory because, being conceived as passive, we may demand that the notion of it shall be realized in the form of passive existence, or ideas, and this demand it cannot fulfill—or if it does, it at once becomes idea, and then Berkeley asks: why reduplicate existence and attempt to think matter otherwise than as it is revealed to us in the percipient consciousness? The notion of matter is thus inadequate to its objective existence. If it be replied that matter is active, produces, brings about effects, Berkeley would say that the notion of activity is indentical with the notion of spirit; for as soon as you attempt to conceive it as matter, you make it passive, i. e., idea, and thus destroy activity. If then you attempt to conceive matter in itself, as an absolute existence apart from spirit, you must admit that it must stand on its own merit, i. e., as passivity, and thus, again, it is idea.

The notion of spirit, however, though 'inadequate' in so far as we attempt to characterize it by conceptions borrowed from passive ideas, is not inconsistent; for the conception of spirit does not demand that it shall be, *in its absolute nature*, expressed in terms of ideas, but that these shall only signify or *represent* spiritual activity, which is by hypothesis different from ideas. Thus we must, from the very notion of matter, demand a complete knowledge of what it is, and it is thus inadequate to the form of representation which its conception requires; while, on the other hand, the notion of spirit is less inadequate inasmuch as it only requires a medium for the expression of itself, viz, notions or representations. We may accordingly be forced to content ourselves with a relative knowledge of mind or spirit, a 'probability,' as Berkeley expresses it, but of matter we can have no knowledge, except as a mind-dependent existence.

The passages which I have transcribed from Berkeley's dialogue do not seem to me to indicate a sole reliance upon the empirical self in support of his idealistic hypothesis. In the self or 'thinking principle' which 'I evidently know by reflection' there is implied the thought of an activity of relation of which we are made aware not only by its empirical manifestations but, also by the universals of reason or 'notions.' Berkeley, as we have before said, does not think of instituting a Kantian inquiry into the principles which must be presupposed in the constitution of experience in order to render it possible. Before Kant's question could arise there was needed Hume's misinterpretation of Berkeley's 'spirit substance' and the subsequent disintegration of the self into abstract sensations. By Kant the self was to be rediscovered, although the foreign 'Somewhat' against which Berkeley so vigorously contended reappeared in the guise of a *ding-an-sich*, thus occasioning the transformation of the self from an ontological into an epistemological unity. Berkeley, on the other hand, who by his less critical and easier method, had seized upon Locke's combining activity of mind, by extending the scope of its activity from the small sphere to which the latter had confined it, viz., ideas of reflection, gradually transforms it into the self, which, by participation in the Infinite Self, or God, is constitutive of the relations that are througout implied in all phenomenal objects.

" At the first thought it seems altogether incongruous and unseemly to connect Kant or his speculation with Berkeley and his philosophy . . . . . . and yet the two are more nearly connected than at first sight would seem to be possible, not merely·by their historic connection through Hume under the law of action and reaction, but by the problem with which both grappled so earnestly, although their solutions vary so widely. We find them in certain particulars nearer than we should at first have suspected. The matter which Berkeley so passionately rejects while he retains the sensations which are all we know, is, as he conceives it, not greatly unlike the Ding-an-sich which Kant so pertinaciously ignores, while he accepts the phenomena, which somehow he holds to be its representation. The time and space which Kant acknowledges as the *forms* and only as the forms of our direct knowledge affirmed or presumed—of sense experiences by an a priori necessity, are accepted by Berkeley as a priori relations, because necessarily involved in the continued activity of God. Kant's categories of our generalized thinking are matched by Berkeley's original notions of relations between ideas which are discerned and affirmed directly by the mind. The ideas, however, which Kant beheld as shivering ghosts through the midst of his timid scepticism, and which he was forced to recognize as real by a faith which he could only say was a make-believe—of God, the soul, and the cosmos,—these were to Berkeley the pillars and foundation of his philosophic faith. While Kant finds in conscience the command to believe in God, because God is needed as a chief of police for the moral universe, Berkeley finds in God the personal foundation and enforcer of duty, because duty is the voice of reason and goodness, which are but other names for the thoughts and actings of God."

We have endeavored to show that the self of Berkeley is but poorly understood if one fastens upon the category of substance as indicative of his deeper thought or last word about the matter. His unwillingness to apply the category of 'substance,' and his recognition that · being' is an inadequate concept by which to express the self, appear in a few passages in his Commonplace Book. There he says, with regard to the objective source of ideas of sense: "there is a being which wills these perceptions in us," to which he adds: "It should be said, nothing but a Will—a *being* which wills being unintelligible."[1] Likewise he seems to disallow the hypostalization of Will or Understanding, either as modes of a substance, or as faculties in abstraction from the self of which they are different forms of manifestation: "I must not say that will or understanding is all one, but that they are both abstract ideas, i. e., none at all—they not being even *ratione* different from the spirit, *qua* faculties, or active."[2] Again: Thought itself, or thinking, is no idea. "'Tis an act, i. e., volition, as contradistinguished to effects—the Will."[3] Further in his account of the perception of objects, Berkeley says, in a passage already noted in another connection: "when I speak of objects as existing in the mind, or imprinted on the senses, I would not be understood in the gross literal sense—as when bodies are said to exist in a place, or a seal to make an impression on wax. My meaning is only that the minds comprehends or perceives them."[4]

On the whole it does not seem that he has much thought of pressing the analogy of material substance upon his 'active principle.' Although ideas, in so far as they are regarded apart from the relating mind, are passive, and although as coming from a source foreign to the finite mind, the latter is receptive with regard to them; yet ideas in themselves, having no connexion or identity with one another, have a meaning for the finite mind only in so far as the latter possesses the relating activity which is necessary for the interpretation of these significant signs into a rational language. Thus the mind is not a mere *tabula rasa*, a substance-vehicle for conveying into the empirical consciousness a world of ready made perceptions; on the contrary, in so far as empirical perception is present, there is implied the work of rational activity, without which experience would be impossible. The finite mind can interpret the language of the Author of Nature only so far as it possesses the capability of interpretation, i. e., as it shares the rational activity which is at the heart of experience.

With respect to the identity of the finite mind or self, Berkeley is eminently unsuccessful, at least in his early philosophy. The question thus appears to him in the "Commonplace Book": "Wherein consists the identity of persons? Not in actual consciousness, for then I'm not the same person I was this day twelvemonths but while I think of what I did then. Not in potential, for then all persons may be the same for aught I know."[5] Here

---

[1] "Life Letters and Unpublished Writings of Berkeley," p. 430.
[2] Fraser; "Commonplace Book" in "Life, letters, etc.," p. 466.
[3] Ibid, p. 460.
[4] "Third Dialogue between Hylas and Philonious."
[5] Fraser; "Commonplace Book," in "Life, letters, etc.," p. 481.

he seems to rely solely upon memory as the bond of connection between past and present states of consciousness; and its inadequacy as an explanation of any other than empirical identity he could have seen if he had but applied the principles of associational psychology which he himself set afoot.

In the third dialogue between Hylas and Philonous he seems to foresee Hume's subsequent procedure with regard to the self. Hylas says in reply to the long speech of Philonous which we have quoted: "Notwithstanding all you have said . . . . and in consequence of your own principles, it should follow that you are only a system of floating ideas, without any substance to support them. Words are not to be used without a meaning in *spiritual substance* more than in material substance; the one is to be exploded as well as the other,"[1] for "the murder of matter is the suicide of the mind." This objection, suggestive of his Commonplace Book, in which Berkeley says that "the very existence of idea constitutes the Soul "[2] which is a mere 'congeries of perceptions,' is answered as follows: "I know or am conscious of my own being, and that I myself am not my ideas, but somewhat else, a thinking, active principle which perceives, knows, wills and operates about ideas. I know that I, one and the same self, perceive both colors and sonnds: that a color cannot perceive a sound, nor a sound a color: that I am therefore one individual principle, distinct from color and sound; and for the same reason, from all other sensible things and inert ideas. But, I am not in like manner conscious of the existence or essence of Matter."[3] Now from this statement that the self is an individual principle, distinct from ideas, and the preceding assertion that 'Mind is a congeries of perceptions,' it seems that Blakeley contemplated a distinction between an empirical and a rational self, although the distinction is far from being explicitly pointed out.

In the Commonplace book he regards the *person* as immortal, while he denies immortality to the soul, by which he evidently means the self in its individual or empirical aspect. Berkeley's theory of personality is a later development of his philosophy, in the progress of which he has come to place increasing reliance upon the notion, rather than upon mere intuition. But if, in his early theory, he fails to distinguish clearly between the empirical self as a mere congeries of perceptions, and the rational activity which renders possible an interpretation of the sign language of Nature, in the later philosophy of Siris there is a tendency to lose the identity of the self in Universal Mind. He now verges upon

---

[1] "Third dialogue between Hylas and Philonous."
[2] Fraser; "Commonplace Book," "Life, letters, etc.," p. 438.
[3] "Third dialogue between Hilas and Philonous."

mysticism, and draws largely from Neo-Platonic sources for his conceptions. Jamblichus, he says, furnishes a doctrine that "there is a principle of the soul higher than nature, whereby we may be raised to a union with the gods, and exempt ourselves from fate."[1] "According to the Platonic philosophy, *ens* and *unum* are the same. And consequently our minds participate so far of existence as they do of unity. But it should seem that personality is the indivisible center of the soul or mind, which is a monad so far forth as she is a person. Therefore Person is really that which exists, inasmuch as it participates in the Divine unity:"[2] Again, he says: " Upon mature reflection, the person or mind, of all created being, seemeth alone indivisible and to partake most of unity. But sensible things are rather considered as one than truly so, they being in a perpetual flux or succession ever differing and various. Nevertheless, all things together must be considered as one universe, one by the connexion and order of its parts, which is the work of mind, whose unit is, by Platonics, supposed a participation of the first τὸ ἕν."[3] "Aristotle himself, in his third book of the Soul, saith it is the mind that maketh each thing to be one. . . . How this is done Themistius is more particular, observing that as being conferreth essence, the mind, by virtue of her simplicity, conferreth simplicity upon compound beings. And, indeed, it seemeth that the mind, so far forth as person, is individual. Therein resembling the divine one by participation, and imparting to other things what itself participates from above. This is agreeable to the doctrine of the ancients; however the contrary opinion of supposing number to be an original primary quality in things, independent of the mind, may obtain among the moderns."[4]

Here Berkeley in his theory of personality relies upon the concept of unity not only to exhibit the necessary dependence of the finite upon the infinite mind, but also to differentiate the former from the latter. "Number," he now says, in entire agreement with his earlier philosophy, " is no object of sense :" "it is an act of the mind. The same thing in a different conception is one or many."[5] Unity he still regards as a creature of the mind, and not something existing in things independent of the mind; yet it is no longer as formerly an abstract idea, but a notion. And the notions, as we have seen, are in Siris identified with the archetpyes or ideas of Reason, immanent in the phenomena of sense. The latter, as Berkeley insists, are not to be regarded in one aspect

---

[1] "Siris," § 272.
[2] Ibid, § 346.
[3] Ibid, § 350.
[4] Idid, § 356 and 357.
[5] Ibid, § 288.

alone, for the phenomenon is not merely the complex of sensations which has been marked by one name, and so reputed as a Thing. The Thing is, in another aspect, as the presented object of consciousness, an irreducible fact; it must finally be referred to its causal source and receive its ultimate explanation in objective Universal Mind. The identity of the thing is not a mere fictitious identity, for the unity which the mind introduces into sensations has its counterpart in an objective unity whose source is Universal Mind. As the finite mind, in its explanation of phenomena, procedes from synthesis to higher synthesis, by the rediscovery in Time of the archetypal ideas or notions, it becomes aware of the 'Divine unity' in which it participates.

But while *person* is really that which exists, inasmuch as it participates in the Divine Unity, difference is not lost; for it is also true that "the mind so far forth as person is individual." Personality is for Berkeley the most adequate category for the complete explanation of experience, since the self not only expresses the highest synthesis but, true to the empirical aspect of things, it also expresses difference, as self distinguished from self. My experiences, he seems to say, must be referred to a higher source than myself, and there is a cosmical order independent of me; yet, in a very real sense also, these experiences are mine, and I am not the mere theatre for the play of passing phenomena, since in my ability to discern the unphenomenal character which attaches to my experiences, in the significance which the archetypal ideas have for me, my empirical self becomes, like my other phenomenal experiences, the symbol of a higher personality.

But there is another reason why Berkeley, in his final account of the relation of the self to God, rejects a complete identification of the self with God. We have seen that in his early philosophy, Berkeley's conception of God seems unmistakably to be of the deistic cast. The arbitrariness of the divine nature language is chiefly put forward; God is seemingly regarded as an extraneous power working effects in us. But the interpretability of this language rests for us upon the presupposition of a necessary unity of the finite with the Absolute Mind or Reason. "Siris" is the explication of this, and the universals of Reason which formerly received such brief recognition are thé means whereby we arrive at the knowledge of an objective order of things, which as the deeper meaning, is the completion as well as the ground of Berkeley's earlier idealism. With his increasing gnosticism, his growing confidence in the universals of Reason, Berkeley is apparently more tolerant of views which in strictness cannot be called theistic. "Whether the νοῦς be abstracted from the sensible world, and considered by itself as distinct from and presiding over the created system; or whether the whole Universe, including mind, together with the mundane body, is conceived to be God, and the creatures to be partial manifestations of the Divine essence—there is no Atheism in either case, whatever misconception there may be; so long as Mind or Intellect is understood to preside over, govern and conduct the whole frame of things."[1] As we have elsewhere seen, the immanence of the divine Reason in the world of sense is the view which is now favored by Berkeley; but it is not maintained to the exclusion of the theistic view which dominated his early idealism: and in this he avoids the pantheism towards which he seems tending and the complete resolution of the self into an Absolute Reason.[2] It is true that his theistic utterances are no longer dogmatic assertions as formerly. The limitation of that finite knowledge which would grasp the infinite is now more clearly recognized. The theistic conception of God comes as the deeper insight into the ever present creative Reason which informs and maintains the world. It comes as a conviction that as man in his rational activity is made aware of a higher rational self which is the completion of the finite and the presupposition of our knowledge of a world, so may this higher self be more completely known by conceiving it in analogy with the total nature of man. As in Berkeley's idealism, and more expressly in the later form which it takes in "Siris," Reason is not to be absolutely divorced from sense, so neither is Will a faculty distinct from Reason. Not Reason alone, but Reason and Will, as different expressions of man's spiritual activity, constitute his inner self.

In the third dialogue between Hylas and Philonous we have already seen Berkeley's statement that God is to be known only by reflecting upon the self, " by heightening its powers and removing its imperfections." In "Alciphron, the Minute Philosopher," the question of the legitimacy of this process comes up. The inadequacy of finite categories is recognized, while predication by means of them is nevertheless defended by reverting to the scholastic argument that they are applied "by way of eminence and not by way of defect."[4]

The theistic view, which he thus but poorly maintains as against pantheism, is perhaps furnished with a more rational basis if one reads it in connection with his later utterances with respect to the notion, and the function which we found must be assigned

[1] "Siris," § 326.

[2] Cf. "Siris," § 276, 287.

[3] " La large tolérance de Berkeley n'excommunie pas le pantheism, bien qu'elle affirme que le fonds de l'être, en Dieu comme en nous, est l'indivisible unité de la personne." L. Carrau: "La philosophie religieuse en Angleterre;" Paris, 1888, p. 27.

[4] "Divine Visual Language," § 19.

to it in the constitution of experience. Viewed in this light, man's knowledge of God is but the farther extension of his knowledge of the phenomenal order. In the phenomenal world of Berkeley we are not cut off from a world of noumenal existence, for in the sense-material which is subjected to the unifying work of finite conceptions there is nothing foreign to Reason. In the generalizations of science, by means of which is made possible for us an orderly and connected world of experience, nay even in perception itself, we are already transcending the merely phenomenal. Finally, in the highest completed synthesis, the Divine Reason, we have merely the last step which gives meaning to the whole. Man shares in the Universal Reason, and it is only by his participation in this Reason that he is enabled to take cognizance of this Unity, which is the truest explanation of himself and of the world in which he lives. But in man Reason and Will are equally fundamental, alike universal expressions of his experience of himself, and together they constitute his personality. In his conception of God Berkeley refuses to be be content with mere Reason as the final explanation of things. Reason, as so conceived, is scarcely differentiated from Fate, while the Reason it is Berkeley's purpose to discover is a purposeful activity, directed toward the Supreme Good; it is, as he tells us, Will which "conducted and applied by intellect." The Divine arbitrariness is still retained; God is Divine Will directed by Divine Reason. Although in that Reason the finite is now seen to participate, the key to the knowledge of God is not only the rational, but the moral implication contained in man's knowledge of himself.

---

[1] Siris, § 254.

CHAPTER IV.

The relations which obtain either by way of agreement or contrast between the earlier and later phases of Berkeley's idealism, and which have been exhibited somewhat in detail with respect to the three objects of human knowledge,—ideas, relations, and that third class of existences, denominated by Berkeley, spirits, may now be briefly summarized.

With respect to ideas we distinguished between three classes: (1) the sensation; (2) the phenomenal object, which is in one aspect a mere complex of sensations, and which in another aspect remains an objective datum of consciousness, ultimately explained only by reference to the objective mind of God; (3) the archetype or Idea of Reason. The early philosophy of Berkeley exhibits his insistance upon the subjective character of phenomena, while in the later philosophy of "Siris," their objective character is brought to light by means of the immanent universals, ideas, whose existence had in the "Principles" a tacit recognition in the admission that there are universal notions.

Turning to the connection of ideas, we found that in the earlier philosophy the principle of Causality is declared to be inoperative between ideas, as they are here regarded, in their particular and subjective aspect. A custom or habit of relating passively experienced sensations is apparently sufficient to account for the presence of the external phenomenal object. The theory is in the first instance differentiated from the subsequent human traduction of it only in the implicit recognition of the fundamental unity which subsists between the finite and the Divine Mind, in the fact that the former possesses the capability of rationally interpreting the sensation symbols which ultimately depend upon the causal activity of Divine Will. Again, in the "Principles of Human Knowledge" and in the "Dialogues," Berkeley furnished ample acknowledgment of the fact that the phenomenal object, for which he prefers the term 'idea' rather than thing, has not a merely subjective existence, although, he declares it is meaningless if we attempt to conceive it out of all relation to percipient consciousness. His sufficient acknowledgment of this is, however, in this early phase of his idealism, unsupported otherwise than by citing the fact that ideas of sense are apparently independent of human volition, being produced in a regular, orderly and coherent series.

But, as we approach Berkeley's later realistic position, we find him evidently aware that the objectivity of phenomena cannot be established in so simple a way.   Accordingly, in "Alciphron," the objective implications of the phenomenal object are made more expressly the subject of study, which results in the discovery that any perception is not merely the sum of particular sensations, but that, on the contrary, in order to the recognition of any perceived object, there is involved the work of unconscious rational inference.[1] A few sensations serve as signs by which we are led to expect other unperceived sensations, provided certain conditions be fulfilled.   These present sensations are nothing of themselves, but only as they are signs of relations whose permanence and objectivity are due to the constitutive universals of Supreme Mind.[2]   Immediate perception is thus seen to imply mediation; and "faith in an established, objective order of association between the two kinds of sense phenomena (visual and tactual) is the basis of the constructive activity of intellect in all inductive interpretation of sensible things."[3]   Berkeley's association of ideas is, as Fraser points out,[4] not merely subjective but objective, although his position of objective association is not reached critically; it is, says Fraser, his "religious faith in the constancy of the divine constitution of the cosmos."   "Objective association originates the notions of sensations as significant signs, and belief in the invariableness of the relations of which they are significant."   Subjective association, on the other hand, "helps us to recollect the meaning of each particular sensation and connect the signs with their significance in our imagination."[5]

In the latest phase of his idealism, represented by "Siris," we have seen that the 'judgment of suggestion' ripens into the explicit recognition of universals of Reason, or the constitutive notions, imminent in sense.   The legitimacy of Berkeley's final resort to the notion, of which he makes such important use in establishing a more consistent foundation for his early idealism, was found in the fact that his early nominalism was directed merely against the hypostatization of conceptions in abstract separation from mind as percipient, while a more concrete universal was admitted by him even in his early theory, although its function in the constitution of experience was but imperfectly conceived.

Finally, our consideration of Berkeley's third class of existences, viz: Spirits, revealed that, corresponding to Berkeley's growing insight into the nature of the phenomenal object, there

---

[1] Cf. Wenley; "British Thought and Modern Speculation," p. 149 of Scottish Rev., vol. 19.

[2] Fraser; "Philosophy of Berkeley."

[3] Ibid, p. 395.

[4] Fraser; "Philosophy of Berkeley" in "Life, Letters and Unpublished Writings," p. 304.

[5] Ibid, p. 404.

also emerges a theory of the self and God which is more consistent with the rationalism that is implicitly the basis of his theory of the world. That the world is to be regarded as my individual representation, had never been maintained by Berkeley, as some would have us believe. Its ultimate dependence upon Divine, rational will had been affirmed at the outset, the guarantee for its independence of me consisting in the very fact of Berkeley's insistence that perception and conception should not be thought to exist in absolute separation from one another. The particular is indeed the conscious datum to which introspective analysis of the phenomenal object conducts us; but the conceptual existence of the latter is as much a basal fact of consciousness as the particulars by means of which it translates itself into the concrete perceptual experience of individual minds. Accordingly the early theory, which tells us that particular sensations are merely the signs by which we are enabled to interpret the rational language of a supreme Author of Nature, becomes, by means of the later development of the notion, the obverse of Berkeley's rationalistic philosophy, in which we are led to see that the relations which subsist between pheno mena, in the organic system of human experience, are not mere subjective fictions, but objective relations, discoverable by us, because of the essential unity which obtains between the finite and the Universal Mind, upon which these relations ultimately depend.

Yet, as we have seen, in this unity of the self with God, to which he finally conducts us in Siris, difference is not merged in mere identity. The world is also in a sense the representation of the finite self, not because of the mere fact that man is a percipient organism, but rather because of that very unity which obtains between the finite and the infinite in virtue of which man possesses an 'imperishable personality all his own',[1] sharing, as he does, in the universal constitutive ideas. Through man, by means of these universals, the world is constituted, and is representative alike of an eternal or timeless order of things subsisting in the mind of God, though also of the subjective interpretation which man puts upon his experience. From this subjectivity, man, by voluntary willingness of insight into the eternal order, seeks to free himself, and thus reconstitute the world in the likeness of God. Thus the early doctrine that nature is in its totality an interpretable system, dependent upon a Power that is not ourselves, seems borne out in Siris by his theory of the personality or 'spiritual individuality'[2] of man.

It must, however, be kept in mind that the separate strands of Berkeley's philosophy were never united in an organic whole. The

[1] Wenley; "British Thought and Modern Speculation;" Scottish Rev., Vol. 19, p. 154.

[2] Fraser; "Berkeley," p. 207.

manifold implications of the new point of view, consequent upon
his disposal of the fiction of abstract matter, were but imperfectly
conceived. The work of establishing an idealistic philosophy
which should take the place of previous materialistic theories was
only partially sketched, never definitely executed. Furthermore,
his philosophy was always in a state of transition, and accordingly
one cannot regard any particular phase of its development as an
adequate expression of Berkeley's complete thought about reality.
Empiricism, which is by far the dominant principle of his early
theorizing, long ago yielded up to more consistent systematizers
material valuable not alone for psychological method but for general scientific enquiry. On the other hand, the final idealistic
position which he reached in Siris was presented in too fragmentary
a form to be of abiding service to subsequent philosophy.

"Elle n' était pas fausse, mais incomplète" . . . . . . la *Siris* n' est qu' un
développement plein de grandeur de ce que nous ont révélé les premières oeuvres.
Berkeley est arrivé au seuil de la vieillesse, il a lutté jusqu' ici contre ce qu'il croit
le mal et l' erreur; nul polemiste via été plus ardent, plus soupple, plus infatigable;
il a poursuivi dans tous ses retrenchments successifs la matière en soi; il a réfuté
Collins, Mandeville, Shaftesbury, combattu l' étendue-substance de Descartes, la
monade de Leibniz, l' attraction newtonienne et jusqu' un principe du calcul
infinitésimal; c' est encore un soldat de la vérité qu' il est parti pour les Bermudas.
Le voilà dans sa retraite de Cloyne; sa philosophie, comme sa vie, a cessé d' être
militante, il lit et médite, laisse sa pensée poursuivre son ascension de principe en
principe, jusqu' à l' Un suprême; peu soucieux des objections et des preuves,
s' enchantant, sans trop s' interroger sur l' authenticité des textes, des échos de la
sagesse antique, où il croit surprendre comme le souffle affaibli d'une inspiration
sacrée. C' est ainsi que Platon, parvenu au bout de ses jours et au sommet de son
genie, laisse à de plus jeunes les procédés de réfutation, les armes de la dispute,
et, ressuscitant les vieilles doctrines pour leur donner un plus beau sens, expose
plus qu' il ne démontre dans ses oeuvres magistrales et sereines, *le Timé, les Lois.*
Une critique exigeante peut les traiter de romans philosophiques, comme la Siris;
nous croyons qu' elle aurait tort. Quand une grande intelligence a pensé toute sa
vie ce qu' elle a pensé à le fin, en pleine possession d'elle-même, et ce qui doit
nous intéresser le plus, et qui dans la mesure que les productions humaines en sont
capables, doit contenir le plus de vérité." [1]

If, however, Berkeley cannot be regarded as a thorough-going
empiricist, nor yet as a consistent rationalist, the suggestiveness of
his theory as a whole should not on that account be minimized.
His early theory, in which it is claimed that the existence of sensible objects always involves a reference to percipient consciousness, "denotes a faithfulness to experience" [2] that is not without
its value, when corrected by the subsequent view that mere complexes of sensations, actually present in the individual mind, do not
of themselves constitute the substantiality of the object, which is
also a conceptual unity.

But Berkeley's close identification of perception and conception has, because of the imperfect manner in which he explicates

---

[1] L. Carrau; La philosophie religieuse, pp. 18, 20.
[2] Green; Philosophical Works, Vol. I, Intro. § 173.

the rationalistic elements of his philosophy, been the occasion of not a little misunderstanding with regard to his true attitude toward the phenomenal object, which he substitutes for the thing, independent of consciousness. Thus Green, while admitting that "Berkeley knew that pure theism (which he wished to establish) has no foundation unless it can be shown that there is nothing real apart from thought," says that "he failed to distinguish this true proposition—'there is nothing real apart from thought'—from this false one, its virtual contradictory—'there is nothing other than feeling;'" and in substituting simply 'idea' for Locke's 'idea of a thing,' Berkeley failed, Green further tells us, to take "the truer view of thought and its object, as together in essential correlation constituting the real," and "merged both thing and idea in the indifference of simple feeling."[1]

Of course upon this view that Berkeley has reduced thought and its world to simple feeling, objectivity is done away with; and bodies and things, suggested by feeling, are not real, since present sensations are the only reality. But thus "to isolate the phrase, *esse* is *percipi*, more particularly if the *percipi* be held to imply exclusively the perception of a single individual through the medium of his senses only [as Green in the above passages seems to insist] . . . . is to eviscerate Berkeley."[2] For "he does not declare that we can possess a knowledge only of states of our own consciousness,"[3] since mere feeling present in any individual subjective consciousness, apart from the objective conditions which render feeling interpretable is, on Berkeley's theory, an abstraction no less absurd than abstract matter.[4] The *esse* of things indeed implies *percipi*, yet not alone this but *concipi* or *intelligi*. Therefore to isolate the former phrase is not only to neglect the later realistic development of Berkeley's theory, but to substitute an imagined abstraction in place of Berkeley's concrete particular. The substantiality of the world of external existence, as distinct from the images and fancies of the subjective consciousness, is for Berkeley a fact not to be doubted. The mere Being[5] and substantiality of things is the least that can be said about them, and the true question of idealism is not, does matter exist? since the materiality of the world cannot be doubted; but rather what do we *mean* by saying that there is a material world, i. e., what is the truth about matter?

The answer is, that from our thought of the existence of the

[1] Green; Philosophical Works, Vol. I, Intro.

[2] Wenley; British Thought and Modern Speculation, p. 145.

[3] Ibid, p. 154.

[4] Fraser; "Philosophy of Berkeley," in Life, Letters, etc., of Berkeley, p. 371.

[5] It is not uninteresting at this point to compare Berkeley's idea of being with that of Hegel. The former says: "The general idea of Being appeareth to me the most abstract and incomprehensible of all other."—cf. Princip.es of Human Knowledge, § 17.

material object we cannot abstract that very condition which seems necessary to its being, viz., the condition that it shall be an object for perceptual consciousness. But this does not mean that its existence is entirely comprehended in *my* perception of the object; that it is nothing apart from me; but only that perception is a universal and necessary condition of the being of an object. The two have, as it were, a kind of organic relation, and cannot be separated. What is not *for* consciousness, for the passive experience of perception, no less than what is not constituted by thought, is a mere abstraction.

The view that the Berkelian idea is equivalent to mere feeling involves a most ludicrous construction of Berkeley's theory of the object not immediately present in perception. Does Berkeley mean that, in turning my back upon the object, I thereby annihilate it? In this respect at least, as Mr. Wenley has said, "he was not the fool his critics would have had him." For, in the first place, even if the object has an existence only under the condition of sense-perception; if that condition be not fulfilled, we have yet no right to speak of the object being annihilated, for that would mean that we first take the object apart from perceptual consciousness, and then conceive its destruction. If the object has an existence only in relation to some perceptual consciousness, if it gets its meaning only as it is for a percipient subject, then in the absence of its being perceived, we cannot say that the object is *destroyed* and again flashed back into existence when the condition of sense-perception is fulfilled; object would simply be *meaningless* apart from sense-perception.

However, this is to lay exclusive emphasis upon the *percipi*. Upon Berkeley's principles, Fraser says,[1] the thing may be taken to exist, when we are absent from it, in percisely the same way that the thing present to sense exists, i. e., in the one case as in the other, actual sensations signify a conceivable object. The immediate object being rationally constituted, Berkeley does not mean that, in merely thinking of the object not present in my perception, I by this means recreate it, but that, in my thought of the object, I again recognize the universal conditions which now, as at the time when the object was present to my perception, constitute its independence of me. Does he not mean this in the following? "The trees are in the park, i. e., whether I will or no. Let me but go thither and open my eyes by day, and I shall not avoid seeing them."[2] Or again, "bodies do exist whether we think of them or no, they being taken in a two-fold sense; (1) Collections of thoughts, (2) Collections of powers to cause these thoughts. These latter exist, though perhaps *a parti rei* it may be

---

[1] Fraser; "Philosophy of Berkeley in Life Letters and Unpublished Writings," p. 382.
[2] Commonplace Book, p. 474.

one simple perfect power"[1]—which, as we afterward learn, is Supreme Mind.

Green, however, in considering the philosophical idealism of Berkeley in its bearing upon science, says that "if physical truths imply permanent relations Berkeley's theory properly excludes them."[2] Quoting section 58 of the Principles, he explains that this passage meant for Berkeley that the motion of the earth would begin as soon as we were there to see it; while for us it means that it is now going on as an established law of nature which may be collected from the phenomena. This seems, however, to lay too exclusive emphasis upon the accident of sense-perception. What Berkeley means appears rather to be that the 'established rules of nature' are certain permanent conditions of existence which the mind in its conceptual activity is enabled to discover. Our belief in these primary conditions is ultimately grounded upon our belief in Supreme Rational Will, of which these laws or conditions are the expression. Once discovered, I know that the phenomena, which may be subsumed under these laws, actually occur in accordance with them. The earth moves whether I perceive it or not, for in my thought of the motion of the earth, I recognize that the accident of my individual perception is not involved in the objective conditions underlying my presumption that the earth moves.

Still the universal condition, under which the mind arrives at a knowledge of the laws which subsist between phenomena, is that of sense-perception. Conception is only an abstraction from the concrete life of mind or spirit; we have only a relative universal as likewise a relative particular; therefore mere relations or abstract conditions of existence are not to be hypostatized and taken in absolute separation from perceptual consciousness. This is the logic of Berkeley's polemic against 'abstract ideas.' Accordingly the motion of the earth, as also any phenomenal object not present to my perception, must be regarded as being in a certain sense perceived. Nor does this imply for Berkeley the idea of God as a percipient being in a human and anthropomorphic sense, for 'God,' it is said in "Siris," 'has no sensory.'[3] Perception is finally translated into a system of rational relations which are intuited rather than perceived. The world is ultimately a rationally constituted cosmos, whose intelligible relations are at once the creation and the object of Supreme Rational Will or Person. Whatever difficulties attach to this view,—and they are doubtless many, it at least avoids the extreme of the rationalistic view by refusing to regard the ultimate unity, to which experience must be subjected, as a *mere system of relations* apart from the concrete life of conscious personality.

---

[1] "Commonplace Book" in "Life, Letters," etc., p. 486.
[2] Green; Philosophical Works, Vol. I, Introduction.
[3] "Siris;" § 289.

www.ingramcontent.com/pod-product-compliance
Lightning Source LLC
Chambersburg PA
CBHW020253090426
42735CB00010B/1907